THE ACID REFLUX COOKBOOK

JUDE ARSON

Copyright

© Copyright 2023 — All rights reserved.

This document is geared towards providing exact and reliable information regarding the topic and issue covered. The publication is sold with the idea that the publisher is not required to render accounting, officially permitted or otherwise qualified services. If advice is necessary, legal or professional, a practiced individual in the profession should be ordered.

- From a Declaration of Principles, which was accepted and approved equally by a Committee of the American Bar Association and a Committee of Publishers and Associations.

In no way is it legal to reproduce, duplicate, or transmit any part of this document in either electronic means or printed format. Recording of this publication is strictly prohibited, and any storage of this document is not allowed unless with written permission from the publisher. All rights reserved.

The information provided herein is stated to be truthful and consistent in that any liability, in terms of inattention or otherwise, by any usage or abuse of any policies, processes, or directions contained within is the solitary and utter responsibility of the recipient reader. Under no circumstances will any legal responsibility or blame be held against the publisher for any reparation, damages, or monetary loss due to the information herein, either directly or indirectly.

Respective authors own all copyrights not held by the publisher.

The information herein is offered for informational purposes solely and is universal as so. The presentation of the information is without a contract or any type of guaranteed assurance.

The trademarks that are used are without any consent, and the publication of the trademark is without permission or backing by the trademark owner. All trademarks and brands within this book are for clarifying purposes only and are owned by the owners themselves, not affiliated with this document.

Table of Contents

INTRODUCTION 7
What Is Acid Reflux? 7

PREVENTION OF ACID REFLUX 9
Natural Remedies 11
What to Eat for Acid Reflux 11
What to Drink 12
What to Avoid 13

CHAPTER 1
BREAKFAST AND SMOOTHIES 15
1. Blueberry and Spinach Superfood Green Smoothie 15
2. Yogurt and Fruit Parfaits 16
3. Pear, Ginger, and Almond Yogurt Parfait 16
4. Apple and Linseed Porridge 17
5. Acid Reflux Smoothie 17
6. Yogurt Parfait with Pear and Ginger 18
7. Banana Almond Flax Smoothie 18
8. Omega Overnight Oats 19
9. Baked Apples with Cinnamon and Ginger 19
10. Mexican Breakfast Toast 20
11. Banana Breakfast Pudding 20
12. Papaya Breakfast Boat 21
13. Corn Porridge with Maple and Raisins 21
14. Broccoli Omelet 22
15. Apple Pie Overnight Oats 23
16. Heart-Healthy Smoothie 23
17. Kamut Breakfast Porridge 24
18. Magnesium-Boosting Smoothie 24
19. Coconut Flour Cupcakes 25
20. Vanilla Almond Milk 26
21. Almond Pulp Hummus 26
22. Apple Ginger Smoothie 27
23. Apple Almond Smoothie 27
24. Cranberry Smoothie 27
25. Cinnamon Berry Smoothie 28
26. Detox Berries Smoothie 28

CHAPTER 2
SNACKS AND APPETIZERS 29
27. Almond Meringue Cookies 29
28. Peanut Butter Cookies 30
29. Blueberry Cherry Crisp 31
30. Roasted Bananas with Brown Sugar-Walnut Glaze 32
31. Maple Syrup and Banana Sauce 32
32. Baked Indian Pudding With Maple Syrup 33
33. Cool Cucumber Soup 33
34. High Protein Kidney Bean Salad 34
35. Lighter Apple and Pear Pie 34
36. Peach and Blueberry Yogurt Cake 35
37. Green Yogurt Kick 35
38. Whole Wheat Donuts 36
39. Zucchini Hummus 36
40. No-Bake Energy Balls 37
41. Basil Avocado Pasta Salad 37
42. Stewed Okra 38
43. Wakame Salad 38
44. Plant-Based Chickpea Quinoa Burgers 39
45. The Grilled Romaine Lettuce Salad 40

CHAPTER 3
FIRST COURSE 41
46. Carrot-Ginger Salad 41
47. Ginger Honeydew Soup 42
48. Squash Soup 42
49. Flank Steak 43
50. Marinated Lamb Steaks 43
51. Mediterranean Pizza 44
52. Oven Blasted Vegetables 44
53. Irish Baked Potato Soup 45
54. Vegan Mexican Cheese Pourable 46
55. Crispy Oven-Baked Chicken Tenders 47
56. Roast Rib of Beef 48
57. Rosemary Broiled Shrimp 48
58. Turkey Stew 49
59. Oat and Chickpea Dumplings 49
60. Lamb Kofta Curry 50
61. Vegetarian Pasta Bakes With Halloumi 51
62. Beetroot and Carrots 51
63. Ginger Snap Beef Stew 52

CHAPTER 4
MAIN COURSE 53
64. Creamy Herb Mushroom Chicken 53
65. Steak With Onion 54
66. Lamb Stew With Olives 55
67. Sweet and Crunchy Coleslaw 55
68. Mediterranean Green Beans 56
69. Summer Vegetable Kebabs 56
70. Baked Potato Soup 57
71. Grilled Vegetable Pasta Salad 57
72. Miso-Glazed Scallops 58
73. Mashed Cauliflower Potatoes 59
74. Zucchini and Carrots Frittata 59
75. Steamer Clams With Bacon and Fennel 60
76. Thai Tofu and Red Cabbage Bowl 61
77. Mushroom Chicken and Rice 62
78. Baked Chicken Thighs 63
79. Chicken Stew 64
80. Edamame Stir Fry 65
81. Ham and Asparagus Quiche Bites 66
82. Baked Chicken Meatballs 67

CHAPTER 5
HEALTHY AND TASTY RECIPES TO ENJOY LIFE WITH YOUR FAMILY AND YOUR FRIENDS 69
Tasty Sunday Lunch 69
83. Mushroom Rice 69
84. Bananas Brulee with Vanilla Cream 70
85. Frozen Watermelon Yogurt Pops 71
86. Honeydew Melon and Cilantro Ice Pops 72
87. Easy Turkey Meatloaf 73
88. Apple and Spinach Salad 73
89. Vanilla Frappe 74
90. Vanilla Ice Cream 74
91. Hamp Seed and Banana Green Smoothie 75
Tasty Dinner with Friends 75
92. Frozen Berry and Gingernut Yogurt Pops 75
93. Chia Seed Pudding 76
94. Immunity-Boosting Soup 77
95. Low Acid Almond Raspberry Cobbler 78
96. Barbecued Rump of Beef in Dijon 79
97. Pasta With Walnut Pesto 79
98. Dill Rye Bread 80
99. Ginger Applesauce 81
100. Maple Pumpkin Custard 82
Tasty Dinner with Family 83

101. Green Pancakes 83
102. Maple Pancakes 84
103. Mashed Parsnips 84
104. Blueberry, Chia, Banana and Spinach Smoothie 85
105. Easy Homemade Vanilla Pudding 86
106. Baked Apples With Tahini Raisin Filling 87
107. Vanilla Parfait 87
108. Pumpkin Pudding Parfaits 88

CHAPTER 6
MEAL PLAN 89

CONCLUSION 91

CONVERSION TABLE 93
VOLUME EQUIVALENTS (LIQUID) 93
VOLUME EQUIVALENTS (DRY) 93
OVEN TEMPERATURES 94
WEIGHT EQUIVALENTS 95

Introduction

What Is Acid Reflux?

Acid reflux is a common digestive disorder that causes irritation, heartburn, pain at the stomach's opening, and burning in the food canal. This problem is caused by the reverse flow of fluid and food from the stomach to the throat. People worldwide suffer from acid reflux and other related issues, which can worsen if not treated promptly and properly. The increased ratio of acid reflux issues, according to health consultants, is due to inappropriate food consumption, poor food options, lack of sleep, stressful mental conditions, and a lack of physical activity in people's daily routines. The digestive system is a sensitive organ that can be easily upset by physical exertion or mental restlessness. A person's productivity and thinking ability can suffer as a result of ongoing gastric issues. Following proper diet plans and implementing exercise routines can aid in reflux treatment and improve digestive health. Acid reflux can easily affect people who are obese, diabetic, or have inflammation issues.

Acid reflux is a common disease that causes a burning discomfort in the lower chest area. This occurs when bowel acid backs up into the food pipe. Usually, acidic and fatty foods can be triggers for acid reflux. When acidic foods hit your stomach, they could immediately trigger acid reflux. This is because acid reflux is the bringing up of acid. Fatty foods have a different effect, but it still leads to bringing acid back up. Fatty foods lower the ant reflux barrier in your gut. This occurrence increases the chance of you having acid reflux.

Prevention of Acid Reflux

As we all know, prevention is preferable to treatment. It is not just a phrase; it is the ultimate solution and escape in all situations. Whatever disease you are suffering from, you must ensure that you implement some of the important preventative measures that will allow you to live a healthy life. When it comes to acid reflux, you have complete control. Certain precautions can help keep your body in good working order. It is not caused by any external virus or infection; rather, it is the result of mismanagement in your daily routine. You can stop or reverse things in the early stages with a little management and care. The acid reflux prevention guide is simple to follow.

Acid reflux prevention is more concerned with your food choices than with hygienic conditions. It is a type of lifestyle problem that can occur and lead to mismanagement of your food, posture, habits, and lifestyle. As a result, in order to avoid further damage to your body, you must adopt some healthy lifestyle choices. You can avoid the factors that can cause acid reflux by using the prevention options, such as heartburn, obesity, depression, drugs, hernia, and many others. Everything in our bodies is interconnected, and you must ensure that your entire body is healthy. Overall, health is something that can help you be successful in life and avoid all major threats and problems.

Food is directly connected to all stomach problems. One of the most important factors in our bodies is the food we eat. All of the minerals and nutrients we get from food aid in our growth. If we do not eat properly or have the proper food that we require, we may develop deficiencies in our bodies. Cycle doctors recommend having the best food and diet plan in general from the start of our lives. In terms of nutrition, everything should be healthy and well-balanced so that the body does not suffer from any deficiencies.

We used to take care of everything in the diet after a child was born. Other nutritional supplements are intended for emergency use when diet alone is ineffective. As a result, to prevent acid reflux, we must first seek assistance from food. It is one of the best resources for managing acid reflux symptoms throughout your life. Food aids in the prevention of acid reflux. It can help treat acid reflux during the initial stage. Food is beneficial if you have had surgery and are attempting to maintain your condition. In short, regardless of your condition, food is the factor that actually helps you keep things under control. The question is how it can assist you and what you can gain from it. In order to prevent acid reflux using food therapy, it is necessary to make a food selection that helps you in the following manner:

- **Reduce acidity:** It is necessary to eat food that reduces acidity, and that does not have an acidic nature. As such, you cannot take coffee, alcohol, citrus, and other foods that increase the acidic ratio in the stomach. By taking the food that reduces acidity and that is lighter in nature will help your stomach to be better and reduce its acidic fluency. Moreover, it will not let the acid reflux in the food pipe or cause burning in the stomach.
- **Provide the best nutrients:** When you are recovering from acid reflux, your stomach is weak, which affects your entire body. You must select foods that are high in nutrients. Make an effort to consume calcium, magnesium, and phosphorus-rich foods. Bananas, apples, and berries help

to reduce acidity. Avoid processed foods with a lot of spices because they can kill the nutrients in the food.

- **Reduce inflammation:** The unlimited spices and sauces we use in our food are primarily responsible for inflammation or burning. To keep your dietary choices light, it is necessary to use mild spices and sauces. Food spices can aggravate the burning sensation while also increasing inflammation. In certain circumstances, you should choose foods with few or no spices. Additionally, choose anti-inflammatory food options to help you reduce overall inflammation in the organs and body.
- **Helps to repair organs:** There are protein-rich foods such as meat, white meat, grains, and sprouts that can repair body cells internally. The continuous acid reflux in the body damages the organs and cells on a large scale. Extra nutrients are required to ensure the proper recovery of these cells and overall health. In this manner, you should select food options that aid in cell repair and make you feel better from the inside out. It will be beneficial to you in the long run.
- **Keep the digestion process lighter:** Some major issues with acid reflux are with digestion. The acid in the stomach is produced to digest food when we eat so much acidic food that the acid's ratio gets higher and causes a reflux. In order to avoid such conditions, it is necessary to eat food that is lighter to digest. It will help the stomach to produce a lesser amount of acid and digest the food easily. Moreover, the food will not be acidic in nature so it will get mixed in the stomach acid and neutralize the overall equation. It is a little science but overall helps to avoid any critical condition that will make you suffer in the future on a larger scale.
- **Lifestyle changes:** In order to prevent acid reflux and have a quick recovery, in addition to controlling your diet, you need to make some lifestyle changes. These changes help bring about quick and effective recovery as well as prevention of the problem. These changes not only help to avoid the acid reflux problem but to have a better life and avoid any further health constraints.
- **Eat healthily:** The first step in making lifestyle changes is to eat healthier foods. Even if you eat processed foods, refined sugar, and other unhealthy foods, make sure to replace them with healthier alternatives. Consumption of these food options should follow an irregular pattern. To avoid such issues and complications, you must prioritize healthy food options.
- **Plan your meals:** Make sure to take your meals on time at specific intervals. Eating too much or having meals with long breaks in between can never be healthy. You need to feed your stomach with a small meal after a specific interval so there will be no acidity in there. The planned interval-based meals will help you on the path toward safe digestion.
- **Get 8 hours of sleep:** Sleep is essential for allowing your food to digest and your stomach to function properly. Make sure you get 8 hours of good, healthy sleep every night. It should be a full 8-hour sleep cycle with no breaks or interruptions. In the case of a partial sleep cycle, you will eventually feel more exhausted and drained.
- **Manage your stress:** Stress and anxiety can actually affect the digestion system of your stomach. It is not ideal for a healthy living if you keep stressing out your body. Make sure that you keep a balance between work life and leisure time to relax and avoid any health complications. A stressful brain affects the overall body functions and can cause acid reflux.
- **Maintain a balance between food options:** Lifestyle changes do not imply giving up food or restricting yourself to a specific type of diet. It all comes down to balancing your food options. You must strike a balance between the food options you desire and those that are available to you. Make sure you choose the right options to help you maintain a healthy balance in your overall intake.
- **Do not sleep immediately after meals:** It is not an ideal habit to sleep or lay down immedi-

ately after having a meal. In such conditions, it is not possible for the stomach to digest the food properly. It increases the chances of acid reflux and acidity in the stomach to a maximum level.
- **Increase physical exertion:** One of the causes of acid reflux is laziness and staying in one place for long periods of time. If you don't get enough physical activity in your daily routine, you're not burning off enough energy. In this case, the stomach acid remains in the stomach and cannot dissolve properly. This can lead to reflux later on. You can reduce your weight and the likelihood of acid reflux by engaging in physical activity.

Natural Remedies

If you require an effective at-home remedy for heartburn, you should give these a try. These remedies may not offer long-term relief, but they can help ease the discomfort. Not all of them may work for you, so give them a try and see which one is the best fit.

- **Baking soda:** Baking soda is a natural acid neutralizer. Please make sure that you are using baking soda and not baking powder. Baking soda is affordable and can be found in almost every grocery store.
- **Aloe juice:** Only available to people with blood type A. Aloe juice is widely available and reasonably priced in most supermarkets. Try to find one that is all-natural and free of preservatives. The fewer ingredients used, the better. To help soothe your esophagus, drink about 12 cups before meals. Aloe water and aloe juice are not the same, so ensure you get the correct one. Aloe water is typically highly diluted and does not have the same effect as pure aloe juice.
- **Ginger tea:** Ginger root has a lot of medicinal properties and can help soothe the stomach. You can either buy a caffeine-free ginger tea or make one on your own. I would suggest making it yourself because you can be sure it is pure ginger and nothing else. There is a simple recipe for ginger tea in the recipe section under the heading "drinks."
- **Banana:** Eating a banana is one of the oldest and most relied-upon methods to ease heartburn. Bananas contain natural antacids. If you start your day by eating a banana, it really helps counteract the effects of acid reflux.

What to Eat for Acid Reflux

Acid reflux is certainly not a pleasant experience. It's simply not ideal. Fortunately, certain foods can help you avoid and relieve acid reflux symptoms. Similarly, there are foods that can cause or aggravate acid reflux. The best thing you can do is learn which foods cause acid reflux and which foods relieve the symptoms. Because everyone is different, some foods that cause acid reflux that are not on this list may exist. You must conduct your own testing and will learn through trial and error.

Begin by including healthy foods and gradually eliminating trigger foods. Keeping a food diary is extremely beneficial in this regard. You can keep track of what you eat each day and which foods may be associated with acid reflux. This will give you a better idea of which foods you should avoid. Not all healthy diet plans or food options are effective enough to aid in the prevention and treatment of acid reflux. You must select specific combinations and safe food options that aid in the reduction of inflammation, burning, and acidity. Furthermore, you must maintain a balance in your food intake for things to be balanced and work properly.

The below foods will help you manage the symptoms of acid reflux. When you feel acid reflux, try to eat one or some of these foods to help you.

- **Vegetables:** We are all aware that vegetables are beneficial to our health. Adding more vegetables to your diet will, in fact, increase the amount of nutrients your body receives. They have a low fat and acid content by nature. Leafy green vegetables, potatoes, cucumber, broccoli, and cauliflower are all good choices.
- **Ginger:** Please don't think you have to eat an entire thumb of ginger. Fortunately, you don't need much of it to reap the benefits. Ginger tea is another option. Ginger is a natural anti-inflammatory food that can help with a variety of gastrointestinal issues.
- **Oats:** Fiber-rich foods are good for your digestive system and can help relieve acid reflux. Oats are simple to prepare and high in fiber. You can easily incorporate it into your diet by eating it with fruit for breakfast.
- **Non-citrus fruit:** Fruit is generally very good for you, so you will do your body good if you increase the amount you eat. Citrus is high in acid, and that is why you should be avoiding those types of fruit. Some of the fruit that you can incorporate into your diet are bananas, apples, melons, and pears.
- **Lean meat and seafood:** The key word here is lean. These types of meats are low in fat and high in protein. Some examples of these foods are seafood, turkey, and chicken. Cooking them by grilling, poaching, and baking is best. Always avoid frying.
- **Egg whites:** Although the entire egg is high in nutrients and protein, the yolk is also high in fat. This may cause acid reflux. Using only the whites is a great way to get your protein without adding fat.
- **Healthy fats:** Good fats can actually help with acid reflux. It is the saturated and trans fats that cause a significant problem. While it is not good to eat large amounts of any fat, healthy fats are packed full of nutrients and can help lessen the symptoms of acid reflux. Sources of healthy fats include avocados, nuts, flaxseed, and olive oil.

What to Drink

We already know that caffeine-rich beverages, highly acidic beverages, and carbonated beverages are bad for acid reflux. However, we haven't discussed the types of drinks you should consume. Take note of this. While you should avoid drinking too many liquids as this may aggravate your acid reflux, many drinks are beneficial to your health.

- **Herbal teas:** Herbal teas are great for aiding digestion and are used for various digestive problems. Chamomile, licorice, and ginger teas are the best for acid reflux. They calm the stomach and can help soothe you. Just remember to avoid mint teas.
- **Smoothies:** Bananas, apples, ginger, and other non-citrus fruits are all excellent choices. Smoothies are easy to digest, easy to swallow, and very refreshing when consumed. A smoothie made with the right ingredients can help with acid reflux symptoms.

- **Fruit juices:** We've already discussed how to avoid citrus fruits in your diet, but citrus isn't the only fruit that makes great juice. Non-citrus fruits can be juiced in large quantities. You can buy them in stores or purchase a juicer and juice your own fruits and vegetables. Carrot, ginger, aloe vera, watermelon, and cucumber are excellent choices.
- **Water:** We should all be getting enough water into our diets. The PH of the water is neutral, which means it can help raise the PH of an acidic meal. Drinking too much water can have adverse effects on acid reflux, so don't overdo it. If you drink when you are thirsty, you should be fine. It is best not to overthink this one.

What to Avoid

There has been some discussion about what foods cause acid reflux. Certain foods, however, have been shown to cause acid problems in many people. You may have noticed that you get heartburn after eating certain foods. While food is not the only cause of acid reflux, it can certainly be a trigger. Avoiding anything that may upset your body is critical to controlling the symptoms. Check out this list of common trigger foods to see if you have any issues with any of them.

- **Fatty foods:** Although this is a broad category, I'm sure a few foods came to mind when you read that. Fried foods, fast foods, full-fat dairy products, and fatty meats are all permitted. Fatty foods cause stomach acid to back up and delay stomach emptying. It is preferable to avoid these foods as much as possible. They usually do more harm than good.
- **Citrus fruit and tomatoes:** These are very acidic fruits and are not suitable for people who suffer from acid-related problems. Do your best to avoid them. Some of the fruit on the list are oranges and pineapples. If you are worried that you won't be able to have a delicious tomato sauce ever again, then take a look at our low-acid tomato sauce in the recipe section.
- **Chocolate:** This is a food that most people would be sad to avoid. Unfortunately, chocolate has been shown to increase acid reflux due to the presence of something called methylxanthine.
- **Spicy food:** These foods will not cause reflux in everyone, but they may cause problems for some. It is best to keep track of what happens to your body after eating foods like this. Sometimes it's the way it's cooked or the dish itself that's the issue, not the entire food category.
- **Caffeine and mint:** It has been reported that some people suffer from acid reflux after they have a cup of coffee or chewed on a piece of mint gum. If you notice this, then try and avoid these two things. Instead, go for caffeine-free coffee and mint-free gum and sweets.

Chapter 1
Breakfast and smoothies

1. Blueberry and Spinach Superfood Green Smoothie

Preparation Time: 5 minutes **Cooking Time:** 0 minutes **Servings:** 1

INGREDIENTS

- 1 medium ripe banana
- 4 large ice cubes
- ½ cup fresh blueberries
- ¼ cup milk replacement
- 1 cup fresh spinach

DIRECTIONS

1. Gather the necessary components.
2. Puree the banana, ice cubes, blueberries, and liquid in a blender until smooth.
3. Blend in the spinach until it is fully smooth and creamy.
4. While no sweetener is required in this recipe since the blueberries carry the flavor and are naturally sweet, if you find the smoothie to be too bland, consider adding a pinch of agave nectar. To integrate, blend until smooth.
5. Serve and enjoy.

Nutrition: Calories: 147 g; Carbs: 28.6 g; Protein: 4.7 g; Fat: 1.6 g.

2. Yogurt and Fruit Parfaits

Preparation Time: 5 minutes   **Cooking Time:** 0 minutes   **Servings:** 4

INGREDIENTS

- 3 cups vanilla nonfat yogurt
- 1 cup fresh or defrosted frozen strawberries in juice
- 1 pint of fresh blackberries, raspberries, or blueberries
- 1 cup good quality granola

DIRECTIONS

1. In the bottom of four tall glasses, layer cup of vanilla yogurt.
2. Mix fresh berries with defrosted strawberries and juice.
3. Layer fruit and granola with yogurt in alternating layers until the glasses are completely filled.
4. To keep the granola crispy, serve parfaits right away.

Nutrition: Calories: 1144 g; Carbs: 146.7 g; Protein: 84.7 g; Fat: 24.8 g.

3. Pear, Ginger, and Almond Yogurt Parfait

Preparation Time: 5 minutes   **Cooking Time:** 0 minutes   **Servings:** 4

INGREDIENTS

- 2 pears
- 3 cups Greek yogurt
- 1 tsp minced ginger
- 2 tsp honey
- ½ cup sliced almonds

DIRECTIONS

1. Pears should be peeled, cored, and diced into small chunks.
2. In a mixing bowl, add the pear and Greek yogurt, along with the ginger, and, if desired, a drizzle of honey.
3. Serve with sliced almonds on top.

Nutrition: Calories: 1504 g; Carbs: 74.5 g; Protein: 63.4 g; Fat: 105.8 g.

4. Apple and Linseed Porridge

Preparation Time: 5 minutes **Cooking Time:** 8 minutes **Servings:** 6

INGREDIENTS

- 100 g porridge oat
- 2 tbsp ground linseed
- ½ tsp ground cinnamon, plus extra for the sprinkling
- 150 ml pot of probiotic yogurt
- 500ml of skimmed milk
- A drizzle of agave syrup or honey
- 2 eating apples, peeled and grated

DIRECTIONS

1. Mix the milk, cinnamon, oats, and apples in a medium saucepan. Bring to a boil, stirring constantly, then reduce to a low setting and simmer for 4 to 5 minutes.
2. Add the ground linseeds and divide them among the four dishes for breakfast. Each one should include a dollop of yogurt, a drizzle of honey or agave syrup, and a dash of cinnamon.

Nutrition: Calories: 973 g Carbs: 153.3 g Protein: 32.6 g Fat: 25.6 g.

5. Acid Reflux Smoothie

Preparation Time: 5 minutes **Cooking Time:** 0 minutes **Servings:** 6

INGREDIENTS

- ¾ cup cashew milk
- ¼ cup fresh spinach
- 1 banana (frozen)
- ½ pear
- ½ inch ginger root
- ⅓ cup rolled oats
- 5 fresh basil (just leaves)

DIRECTIONS

1. Spinach, cashew milk, and basil leaves should all be mixed well.
2. Add the other ingredients and mix well.
3. Serve your smoothie over ice for a cool, refreshing treat.

Nutrition: Calories: 268 g Carbs: 47.3 g Protein: 7.8 g Fat: 5.4 g.

6. Yogurt Parfait with Pear and Ginger

Preparation Time: 10 minutes **Cooking Time:** 0 minutes **Servings:** 1

INGREDIENTS

- 12 gingernut biscuits gingersnaps
- 800 g plain yogurt
- 400 g tinned pears
- 1 tsp crystallized ginger

DIRECTIONS

1. Drain the pears and set aside the juice. Pears should be diced into 1cm pieces.
2. Arrange pears at the bottom of each of the four glasses. A layer of yogurt and a gingernut cookie should be placed on top. On top of the gingernut biscuit, drizzle a tiny bit of the saved juice.
3. Continue layering the pear yogurt and gingernut biscuits, concluding with a yogurt layer on top.
4. Refrigerate for 4 hours or overnight.
5. To serve, garnish the yogurt parfaits with gingernut cookies, cookie crumbs, or fresh pear slices crystallized with ginger.

Nutrition: Calories: 2619 g Carbs: 240.4 g Protein: 64.9 g Fat: 155.3 g

7. Banana Almond Flax Smoothie

Preparation Time: 10 minutes **Cooking Time:** 0 minutes **Servings:** 1

INGREDIENTS

- 1 medium or large banana, cut
- ⅔ cup buttermilk, yogurt, or almond milk
- 1 tbsp roasted unsalted almond butter
- 1 tbsp flaxseeds
- 1 tsp honey or agave nectar
- 1 to 2 drops of almond or vanilla extract

DIRECTIONS

1. If the bananas aren't frozen, put everything in a blender, including ice cubes. Blend well.

Nutrition: Calories: 481 g Carbs: 47.2 g Protein: 12.3 g Fat: 26.9 g

8. Omega Overnight Oats

Preparation Time: 10 minutes   **Cooking Time:** 0 minutes   **Servings:** 1

INGREDIENTS

- 2 cups old-fashioned rolled oats
- 2 cups dairy milk or unsweetened non-dairy milk
- 1 cup plain Greek or non-dairy yogurt
- 3 tbsp maple syrup or honey
- 1 tbsp chia seeds (optional)
- ¼ tsp ground cinnamon
- ¼ tsp kosher salt
- **Optional toppings:** fruits, nuts, seeds, nut butter

DIRECTIONS

1. Mix all the ingredients.
2. Stir everything together until it's completely smooth.
3. Split the oats into individual jars at this point. Refrigerate for at least four hours after covering.
4. Serve with chosen toppings after a final stir.

Nutrition: Calories: 950 g Carbs: 146.5 g Protein: 46.5 g Fat: 19.6 g

9. Baked Apples with Cinnamon and Ginger

Preparation Time: 10 minutes   **Cooking Time:** 40 minutes   **Servings:** 4

INGREDIENTS

- 4 apples
- 2 ginger, chopped
- ½ tsp cinnamon
- 4 prunes, chopped
- 50 g muscovado sugar
- 1 tbsp butter
- 4 scoops of vanilla ice cream for serving

DIRECTIONS

1. Preheat the oven to 200°F. Cut a quarter of each apple and set them into a baking dish.
2. Add ginger, cinnamon, sugar, prunes, and butter in a bowl, and mix well. Pour the mixture over the apples and put the butter on each apple's top.
3. Bake them for 35 minutes or until cooked well.
4. Remove and serve the hot baked cinnamon apple with a scoop of vanilla ice cream.

Nutrition: Calories: 978 g Carbs: 183.1 g Protein: 6.2 g Fat: 24.5 g

10. Mexican Breakfast Toast

Preparation Time: 5 minutes **Cooking Time:** 20 minutes **Servings:** 2

INGREDIENTS

- 2 slices of sprouted bread, toasted
- 2 tbsp hummus
- ½ cup spinach, chopped
- ¼ red onion, sliced
- ½ cup sprouts
- 1 avocado, thinly sliced
- ¼ tsp Himalayan salt
- 1 cup yogurt
- 3 tbsp unsweetened yogurt
- ½ lime, juiced
- 1 tsp cumin
- 1 tsp cayenne

DIRECTIONS

1. In a small bowl, prepare the spicy yogurt by combining all the spicy yogurt ingredients and whisking well to combine.
2. Place toast slices on plates and spread 1 tbsp of hummus on each. Place spinach on each piece and spicy yogurt, red onion, sprouts, and avocado; sprinkle each with salt and serve.

Nutrition: Calories: 916 g Carbs: 62.3 g Protein: 32.4 g Fat: 59.7 g

11. Banana Breakfast Pudding

Preparation Time: 5 minutes plus 8 hours of chill time **Cooking Time:** 0 minutes **Servings:** 1

INGREDIENTS

- 1 cup coconut milk
- 1 tbsp raw honey
- ½ tsp vanilla extract
- ¼ tsp cinnamon
- ⅛ tsp Himalayan salt
- 2 tbsp chia seeds
- 1 banana, sliced
- 1 tbsp walnuts, toasted and crushed
- 1 tbsp cacao nibs

DIRECTIONS

1. Place coconut milk, honey, vanilla, cinnamon, salt, and chia seeds in a small bowl or jar with a cover.
2. Let sit in the fridge, covered, overnight.
3. In the morning, top with banana, walnuts, and cacao nibs before serving.

Nutrition: Calories: 904 g Carbs: 53 g Protein: 16.3 g Fat: 68.8 g

12. Papaya Breakfast Boat

Preparation Time: 5 minutes **Cooking Time:** 0 minutes **Servings:** 2

INGREDIENTS

- 1 papaya, cut lengthwise in half and seeds removed
- 1 cup unsweetened yogurt
- 1 lime, zested
- 3 tbsp raw oats
- 1 tbsp unsweetened shredded coconut
- ½ banana, sliced
- ¼ cup raspberries
- 1 tbsp walnuts, chopped
- 1 tsp chia seeds
- 1 tsp raw honey

DIRECTIONS

1. Place papaya halves on plates and place yogurt on top of each.
2. Then top each half with lime zest, oats, coconut, banana, raspberries, walnuts, and chia seeds.
3. Drizzle with honey and serve.

Nutrition: Calories: 702 g Carbs: 98.2 g Protein: 21.8 g Fat: 24.7 g

13. Corn Porridge with Maple and Raisins

Preparation Time: 5 minutes **Cooking Time:** 0 minutes **Servings:** 2

INGREDIENTS

- ¾ cup cornmeal
- 2 ¼ cup water, divided
- 1 tbsp salt
- 1 tbsp pure maple syrup
- 3 tbsp raisins

DIRECTIONS

1. Whisk together the cornmeal and ¾ cup of water in a small bowl.
2. Bring the remaining 1 ½ cups of water and salt to a boil over medium-high heat in a small pot.
3. Whisk in the cornmeal slurry. Cook, stirring for 10 to 12 minutes, until thick.
4. Stir in the maple syrup and raisins. Then serve hot.

Nutrition: Calories: 530 g Carbs: 117.8 g Protein: 8.7 g Fat: 2.7 g

14. Broccoli Omelet

Preparation Time: 10 minutes   **Cooking Time:** 40 minutes   **Servings:** 4

INGREDIENTS

- 4 to 5 eggs
- 6 to 7oz fresh broccoli crowns or frozen broccoli florets
- 2.5 oz sour cream or unsweetened yogurt
- 2 oz shredded cheddar
- Small bunch of fresh parsley and dill
- 1 tbsp salt
- 1 tbsp butter

DIRECTIONS

1. Butter the middle and sides of an oven-safe frying pan.
2. Bring a saucepan of water to a boil, then drop broccoli into it (if using fresh broccoli, split it into florets before cooking), and simmer for 2 to 3 minutes. Remove the broccoli from the pan and wipe it dry with a paper towel.
3. In a mixing bowl, crack eggs and season with salt as needed.
4. And use a hand mixer; beat the eggs until they have a bubbly feel and have considerably increased volume. Add sliced broccoli to the mix.
5. Add fresh parsley and dill, chopped—also shredded cheddar cheese.
6. Fill with sour cream (or yogurt). Mix everything—Preheat the oven to 380°F.
7. Place the mixture in the prepared skillet or pan and bake in a preheated oven for 20 to 25 minutes. Start checking readiness with a wooden toothpick at the 20-minute mark (it should come out clean and dry when inserted into the center of the omelet); remove the pan from the oven once ready. Serve it sliced up.

Nutrition: Calories: 844 g Carbs: 8.6 g Protein: 52.9 g Fat: 66.6 g.

15. Apple Pie Overnight Oats

Preparation Time: 10 minutes   **Cooking Time:** 0 minutes   **Servings:** 4

INGREDIENTS

- cup old fashioned quaker oats
- 1 tbsp ground cinnamon for serving
- ½ tsp maple syrup
- ¼ cup fat-free vanilla Greek yogurt
- 3 apples diced
- 2 pecans chopped
- ¼ cup milk of any kind
- 1 tbsp chia seeds, can omit if desired

DIRECTIONS

1. In a mason jar, layer the oats first, then the chia seeds, and then pour milk over everything. Combine yogurt, maple syrup, and apple pie spice in a mixing bowl. Pour over the chia and oats.
2. After sealing the Mason jar lid, place it in the refrigerator for 6 to 8 hours. Stir the ingredients together to mix them. Use maple syrup or another sweetener to alter the sweetness as needed.
3. 3. Top with cinnamon, apple slices and chopped walnuts.

Nutrition: Calories: 500 g Carbs: 79.4 g Protein: 13.7 g Fat: 14.4 g

16. Heart-Healthy Smoothie

Preparation Time: 10 minutes   **Cooking Time:** 0 minutes   **Servings:** 4

INGREDIENTS

- 1 Brae burn apple or organic apple
- 1 cup dandelion greens
- ¼ cup Brazil nuts
- 1 cup homemade walnut milk
- ½ tbsp date sugar
- 1 cup blueberries

DIRECTIONS

1. In a blender, combine all the ingredients.
2. Enjoy.

Nutrition: Calories: 587 g Carbs: 61.7 g Protein: 16.5 g Fat: 30.4 g

17. Kamut Breakfast Porridge

Preparation Time: 10 minutes   **Cooking Time:** 40 minutes   **Servings:** 4

INGREDIENTS

- 1 cup kamut
- 4 tbsp agave syrup
- ¾ cup homemade walnut milk
- ½ tsp sea salt
- 1 tbsp coconut oil

DIRECTIONS

1. Using a high-speed blender or food processor, grind the kamut until you have approximately ¼ cups of cracked kamut.
2. In a medium saucepan, stir the sea salt, coconut or walnut milk, and crushed kamut.
3. Boiling should be done over a strong heat. Turn down the heat to medium-low and simmer for approximately 10 minutes, occasionally stirring, until the mixture is the right consistency.
4. Get out of the blaze. Add the agave syrup and coconut oil after that; add fresh fruit as a garnish if necessary.
5. The kamut porridge is delicious.

Nutrition: Calories: 1044 g Carbs: 184.8 g Protein: 27.1 g Fat: 22 g

18. Magnesium-Boosting Smoothie

Preparation Time: 10 minutes   **Cooking Time:** 0 minutes   **Servings:** 4

INGREDIENTS

- 1 cup fresh spring water
- 2 strawberries
- ¼ cup Brazil nuts
- ½ cup figs
- ½ burro banana

DIRECTIONS

1. In a high-quality blender, thoroughly combine all the ingredients.
2. If you think the mixture is too thick, add additional water.
3. Enjoy.

Nutrition: Calories: 263 g Carbs: 15.7 g Protein: 5.9 g Fat: 19.5 g

19. Coconut Flour Cupcakes

Preparation Time: 10 minutes **Cooking Time:** 40 minutes **Servings:** 4

INGREDIENTS

- ½ cup coconut flour
- 2 tsp baking powder
- 1 cup peeled and finely chopped zucchini
- ¼ tsp sea salt
- 4 large eggs
- cup coconut sugar
- 1 tbsp vanilla extract

DIRECTIONS

1. 350°F should be the oven's temperature.
2. Ten cupcake liners should be used to line a regular muffin pan.
3. Mix the zucchini, eggs, vanilla, coconut sugar, coconut flour, coconut flour, salt and baking powder in a blender. Mix until it becomes a smoothie, eggs, vanilla, coconut sugar, coconut flour, salt, and baking powder. Blend until it becomes smooth. If you don't have a good blender, first blend the eggs and the zucchini until they are smooth. After that, add the other ingredients and stir once more.
4. Fill each of the 10 cupcake liners with the batter. Bake at 350°F for 25 minutes. With the use of a tool, you must make sure that the centers of the cupcakes are solid.
5. A cupcake should cool completely before icing and serving. These cupcakes may be kept in an airtight container in the refrigerator for a maximum of 5 days if you want to serve them later.

Nutrition: Calories: 1378 g Carbs: 135.6 g Protein: 41.1 g Fat: 74.6 g

20. Vanilla Almond Milk

Preparation Time: 10 minutes   **Cooking Time:** 0 minutes   **Servings:** 4

INGREDIENTS

- 1 cup raw almonds that have been soaked for six to eight hours
- 2 tsp vanilla extract
- 4 cups filtered water
- tsp sea salt
- 4 pitted Medjool dates

DIRECTIONS

1. Drain the soaked almonds and rinse, then pour them with four cups of fresh water into a high-powered blender. Blend them, so they're creamy.
2. Pour the blended milk into a fine mesh strainer or almond milk bag. To ensure you remove all the liquid from the pulp, press well.
3. Take the strained milk back into the blender. Then add the vanilla, dates, and sea salt to the mixture. Mix until the dates are properly ground. You can change the flavor by tasting.
4. Then move the milk to a container for storage. You should quickly serve the milk or cool it in the fridge till it's ready for use.

Nutrition: Calories: 1262 g Carbs: 72.5 g Protein: 37.2 g Fat: 83.4 g

21. Almond Pulp Hummus

Preparation Time: 10 minutes   **Cooking Time:** 0 minutes   **Servings:** 4

INGREDIENTS

- ½ cup raw tahini
- 1 scant cup wet almond pulp
- 1 tbsp ground cumin
- ½ tsp sea salt
- ¼ cup extra virgin olive oil
- ¼ cup water

DIRECTIONS

1. Combine the salt, tahini, cumin, and olive oil in a high-quality blender.
2. Blend the ingredients well.
3. Add the water and the almond pulp.
4. Then blend it one more time until it is smooth. For improved flavor, keep the hummus in the fridge for an extra 2 hours before serving.

Nutrition: Calories: 2258 g Carbs: 62.6 g Protein: 56.1 g Fat: 198.1 g

22. Apple Ginger Smoothie

Preparation Time: 10 minutes **Cooking Time:** 0 minutes **Servings:** 1

INGREDIENTS

- 1 apple, peeled and diced
- ¾ cup (6 oz) coconut yogurt
- ½ tsp ginger, freshly grated

DIRECTIONS

1. Add all the ingredients to a blender.
2. Blend well until smooth.
3. Refrigerate for 2 to 3 hours.
4. Serve.

Nutrition: Calories: 234 g Carbs: 34.8 g Protein: 7 g Fat: 7.4 g

23. Apple Almond Smoothie

Preparation Time: 10 minutes **Cooking Time:** 0 minutes **Servings:** 1

INGREDIENTS

- 1 cup apple cider
- ½ cup coconut yogurt
- 4 tbsp almonds, crushed
- ¼ tsp cinnamon
- 1 cup ice cubes

DIRECTIONS

1. Add all the ingredients to a blender.
2. Blend well until smooth.
3. Serve.

Nutrition: Calories: 493 g Carbs: 33.1 g Protein: 13.3 g Fat: 27.8 g

24. Cranberry Smoothie

Preparation Time: 10 minutes **Cooking Time:** 0 minutes **Servings:** 1

INGREDIENTS

- 1 cup cranberries
- ¾ cup almond milk
- ¼ cup raspberries
- 2 tsp fresh ginger, finely grated

DIRECTIONS

1. Add all the ingredients to a blender.
2. Blend well until smooth.
3. Serve with fresh berries on top.

Nutrition: Calories: 149 g Carbs: 24.8 g Protein: 3.5 g Fat: 4.1 g

25. Cinnamon Berry Smoothie

Preparation Time: 10 minutes   **Cooking Time:** 0 minutes   **Servings:** 1

INGREDIENTS

- 1 cup frozen strawberries
- 1 cup apple, peeled and diced
- 2 tsp fresh ginger
- 3 tbsp hemp seeds
- 1 cup water
- ½ lime juiced
- ¼ tsp cinnamon powder
- ⅛ tsp vanilla extract

DIRECTIONS

1. Add all the ingredients to a blender.
2. Blend well until smooth.
3. Serve with fresh fruits

Nutrition: Calories: 320 g Carbs: 48.6 g Protein: 6.9 g Fat: 10.6 g

26. Detox Berries Smoothie

Preparation Time: 10 minutes   **Cooking Time:** 0 minutes   **Servings:** 1

INGREDIENTS

- 3 peaches, cored and peeled
- 5 blueberries
- 5 raspberries
- 1 cup alkaline water

DIRECTIONS

1. Add all the ingredients to a blender.
2. Blend well until smooth.
3. Serve with fresh kiwi wedges.

Try these smoothies and improve your acid reflux condition!

Nutrition: Calories: 140 g Carbs: 29.8 g Protein: 4 g Fat: 0.7 g

Chapter 2
Snacks and Appetizers

27. Almond Meringue Cookies

Preparation Time: 25 minutes   **Bake:** 30 minutes /batch + cooling   **Servings:** about ½ dozen

INGREDIENTS

- 4 large egg whites
- ½ tsp cream of tartar
- ½ tsp almond extract
- ¾ cup confectioners' sugar
- ½ cup sugar
- cup ground almonds
- ¼ cup finely chopped almonds

DIRECTIONS

1. In a mini mixing dish/bowl, whisk together the egg whites and cream of tartar, and extract until soft peaks form. Mix the confectioner's sugar and sugar in a mixing bowl. 1 tbsp at a time, add to egg white mixture, and beat on high until stiff glossy peaks form and sugar is dissolved. Fold in the ground almonds gently.
2. Cut a tiny hole in the corner of a pastry bag and insert a #8-star tip. Fill the bag halfway with the egg white mixture. 1-¼-inch-diameter biscuits are piped onto parchment-lined baking pans and topped with chopped almonds.
3. Preheat the oven to 275°F and bake for 30 to 35 minutes or until firm to the touch. Cool thoroughly on wire racks after removing from pans. Keep the container sealed.

Nutrition: Calories: 1449 g Carbs: 216.2 g Protein: 37.5 g Fat: 47.5 g

28. Peanut Butter Cookies

Preparation Time: 10 minutes **Cooking Time:** 30 minutes **Servings:** 4

INGREDIENTS

- 1 egg
- 1 cup brown sugar
- 1 cup peanut butter

DIRECTIONS

1. To start this recipe, turn on the oven and let it heat up to 350°F. While the oven is warming up, take out a baking sheet that you want to use and top it with some parchment paper.
2. You can then take out a medium bowl and add the egg, brown sugar, and peanut butter you choose. Cream these together until you get all the ingredients to mix well.
3. After this, spoon the cookie batter into six portions onto that baking sheet, giving them room to grow and expand.
4. Add the cookies into the oven to bake for a little bit. You want to allow the bottoms to have time to brown as well.
5. After about 6 to 8 minutes, the cookies should be done. Take them out of the oven and give them some time to cool before serving.

Nutrition: Calories: 2625 g Carbs: 267.1 g Protein: 65.2 g Fat: 144 g

29. Blueberry Cherry Crisp

Preparation Time: 5 minutes	**Cooking Time:** 35 minutes	**Servings:** 8

INGREDIENTS

- 1 cup old-fashioned oatmeal
- ⅓ cup coconut flour
- ½ cup chopped macadamia nuts
- 2 tbsp coconut oil
- 3 tbsp almond butter
- 2 tbsp honey
- 1 tbsp cinnamon
- ⅛ tsp sea salt
- 4 cups frozen cherries, thawed
- 2 cups frozen blueberries

DIRECTIONS

1. Set the oven to 375°F. Almond butter in a 9x9 inch glass dish.
2. Mix oatmeal with nuts and flour in a glass bowl.
3. Heat honey in a pan with almond butter, coconut oil, sea salt, and cinnamon.
4. Cook for 3 minutes on low heat while stirring.
5. Gradually stir in the oatmeal mixture and keep mixing well.
6. Spread the blueberries and cherries in the glass dish.
7. Add the oatmeal mixture to the dish and spread it evenly.
8. Bake for 35 minutes until bubbly.
9. Serve.

Nutrition: Calories: 2894 g Carbs: 289.9 g Protein: 64.9 g Fat: 163.8 g

30. Roasted Bananas with Brown Sugar-Walnut Glaze

Preparation Time: 10 minutes **Cooking Time:** 15 minutes **Servings:** 5

INGREDIENTS

- ⅓ cup packed brown sugar
- 2 tbsp reduced-calorie margarine, melted
- ¼ tsp ground cinnamon
- 4 large firm ripe bananas (about 1 and ½ lbs)
- Cooking spray
- ¼ cup chopped walnuts, toasted
- 1 ½ cup vanilla low-fat frozen yogurt

DIRECTIONS

1. Set the oven's temperature to 450°F.
2. Mix the first four ingredients in a bowl, then set aside.
3. Cut the bananas in half lengthwise. Put the cut sides of the banana halves on a jelly roll pan that has been sprayed with cooking spray. Bake for about 4 minutes after 450°F. After evenly coating the banana halves with the sugar mixture, sprinkle the toasted walnuts on top. Bake for 3 more minutes. Every banana slice needs to be divided crosswise into thirds. Serve bananas with any remaining sugar mixture drizzled over the frozen yogurt.

Nutrition: Calories: 1828 g Carbs: 323.2 g Protein: 25.8 g Fat: 47.9 g

31. Maple Syrup and Banana Sauce

Preparation Time: 10 minutes **Cooking Time:** 5 minutes **Servings:** 5 to 12

INGREDIENTS

- ¼ cup butter
- ¼ cup brown sugar
- ½ cup maple syrup
- 2 dashes ground cinnamon
- 3 bananas, sliced

DIRECTIONS

1. Melt the butter in a pan over medium heat. Stir in the brown sugar, syrup, and cinnamon for 2 to 3 minutes or until the sugar melts. Banana slices are then added and heated for 1 to 2 minutes.

Nutrition: Calories: 1225 g Carbs: 186 g Protein: 5 g Fat: 51.3 g

32. Baked Indian Pudding With Maple Syrup

Preparation Time: 10 minutes **Cooking Time:** 2 hours 20 minutes **Servings:** 8

INGREDIENTS

- 4 cups hot milk
- ½ cup yellow cornmeal
- ½ cup maple syrup
- ⅓ cup packed brown sugar
- ¼ cup molasses
- 2 eggs, lightly beaten
- 2 tbsp butter, melted
- 1 tsp salt
- ¾ tsp ground ginger
- ¼ tsp ground cinnamon
- ½ cup cold milk

DIRECTIONS

1. Place the top of a double boiler over low heat and add 4 cups of heated milk. Cook for about 20 minutes, stirring frequently, or until the cornmeal has thickened. Every now and then, stir.
2. Heat the oven to 300°F. Use cooking spray to grease a 2-quart round baking dish.
3. In a large mixing bowl, combine maple syrup, brown sugar, molasses, eggs, melted butter, salt, ginger, and cinnamon. Stir the cornmeal-milk mixture thoroughly before adding it to the baking dish that has been prepared. Over the pudding, pour half a cup of cool milk.
4. The top should be firm but a little tangy after baking for about 2 hours. 30 minutes should pass before serving.

Nutrition: Calories: 2004 g Carbs: 291.6 g Protein: 50.1 g Fat: 70.9 g

33. Cool Cucumber Soup

Preparation Time: 10 minutes **Cooking Time:** 0 minutes **Servings:** 1

INGREDIENTS

- 2 tbsp fresh dill
- ½ cup half-and-half cream
- 2 medium cucumbers
- 1 tbsp fresh dill sprigs for the garnish (optional)
- cup water
- cup sour cream
- ¼ tsp salt

DIRECTIONS

1. Peeling and seeding cucumbers are required. You should mince the dill.
2. In a blender, combine all ingredients and blend until smooth.
3. Until you are ready to serve, cover, and chill.
4. Use fresh dill sprigs as a garnish if you prefer.

Nutrition: Calories: 360 g Carbs: 14.3 g Protein: 7 g Fat: 30.5 g

34. High Protein Kidney Bean Salad

Preparation Time: 10 minutes   **Cooking Time:** 7 minutes   **Servings:** 1

INGREDIENTS

- ¾ cup cottage cheese (crumbled)
- 1 can of kidney beans
- 1 tsp cumin
- ½ lime (juiced)
- 2 tbsp olive oil
- ½ can of sweet corn
- 1 tsp mustard
- 1 tsp honey
- ½ tsp oregano, dried
- 1 tbsp salt
- 1 green onion
- ½ cucumber (finely diced)
- ½ cup parsley or cilantro, fresh

DIRECTIONS

1. Rinse and drain corn and kidney beans before using.
2. You should dice the cucumber and chop the parsley or cilantro.
3. After that, chop the green onion. Everything has gone without a hitch thus far.
4. Put everything that has been rinsed and chopped into a sizable mixing bowl. Now combine everything thoroughly in the cottage with the crumble.
5. Combine all of the dressing's ingredients in a small bowl. Stir and taste to ensure that everything is in order.
6. Once the dressing has been given the all-clear, toss the salad with it.
7. You can now eat your salad.

Nutrition: Calories: 1305 g Carbs: 155.3 g Protein: 44.9 g Fat: 56 g

35. Lighter Apple and Pear Pie

Preparation Time: 20 minutes   **Cooking Time:** 40 minutes   **Servings:** 6

INGREDIENTS

- 6 apples
- 4 pears
- 3 tbsp syrup
- 1 tbsp corn flour
- 4 pastry sheets
- 4 tsp rapeseed oil
- 25 g almond

DIRECTIONS

1. Take a pan, add apples and pears with water and syrup, and cook for 5 minutes.
2. Remove the fruit, pour it into a pie dish, and cook the remainder for another 5 minutes.
3. Mash the remaining fruits into a mixer until smooth, and the syrup is consistent. Cook that syrup for another 4 to 5 minutes, and then pour it into a pie dish.
4. Set the pastry sheets in the dish and brush oil on the top. Bake it for 30 minutes in a preheated oven at 356°F until it turns brown and is cooked. Serve immediately!

Nutrition: Calories: 3219 g Carbs: 419.4 g Protein: 34.2 g Fat: 156.1 g

36. Peach and Blueberry Yogurt Cake

Preparation Time: 20 minutes **Cooking Time:** 1 hour **Servings:** 10

INGREDIENTS

- 1 ½ cup all-purpose flour
- 1 tsp baking powder
- ½ tsp baking soda
- 2 oz butter
- 1 cup sugar
- 2 eggs
- ½ tsp vanilla
- ½ cup yogurt
- 2 peaches, sliced
- 6 oz blueberries
- 1 tsp sugar

DIRECTIONS

1. Grease the baking pan with parchment paper and set aside.
2. Preheat the oven to 350°F.
3. Take a bowl, and add flour, baking powder, and soda. Whisk eggs, butter, and sugar in a separate bowl until fluffy.
4. Now add vanilla extract and Greek yogurt and continue beating until well combined and the texture becomes smooth. Pour the mixture into a floured bowl and mix until well combined.
5. Pour the batter into the baking pan, set the slices of peach, and sprinkle blueberries with sugar. Bake it for 30 to 35 minutes or until golden brown.
6. After baking, let it cool down for 30 minutes and serve with the yogurt topping.

Nutrition: Calories: 1847 g Carbs: 292.7 g Protein: 29.1 g Fat: 62 g

37. Green Yogurt Kick

Preparation Time: 10 minutes **Cooking Time:** 0 minutes **Servings:** 1

INGREDIENTS

- ½ gala apple
- ½ cup spinach
- ½ banana
- ¾ cup yogurt
- ¼ cup cubed papaya

DIRECTIONS

1. Peel and core the apple and then chop it into smaller pieces.
2. Place the apple and the other ingredients in the bowl of your blender.
3. Blend for a minute or until smooth.
4. Serve immediately and enjoy.

Nutrition: Calories: 235 g Carbs: 32.7 g Protein: 8.5 g Fat: 7.7 g

38. Whole Wheat Donuts

Preparation Time: 5 minutes **Cooking Time:** 15 minutes **Servings:** 6

INGREDIENTS

- ¾ cup almond milk
- 1 cup whole wheat flour
- 2 tbsp sugar
- 2 tsp cocoa powder
- ½ tsp baking powder
- ½ tsp baking soda
- ½ tsp salt
- ½ tbsp flax seed
- 2 tbsp oil
- 1 cup sugar, powdered
- 1 tsp vanilla extract
- 1 tbsp milk

DIRECTIONS

1. Preheat the oven to 350°F and set the doughnut baking tray. Put the almond milk in a small bowl and set aside for 5 minutes.
- Add flour, flaxseed, sugar, cocoa powder, vanilla extract, baking powder, baking soda, salt, and oil to a bowl, and mix them well.
2. Now pour the almond milk into it until combined. Pour the batter over the doughnut baking tray and bake for 10 to 13 minutes or until fluffy and cooked.
3. Remove them and let them cool down. Sprinkle powdered sugar or milk.

Nutrition: Calories: 1523 g Carbs: 254.2 g Protein: 19 g Fat: 46.6 g

39. Zucchini Hummus

Preparation Time: 15 minutes **Cooking Time:** 20 minutes **Servings:** 5

INGREDIENTS

- Salt
- 1 tsp chopped dill, fresh
- 1 tbsp tahini
- 1 tbsp olive oil
- 1 chopped zucchini

DIRECTIONS

1. To start this recipe, set it up with a food processor or blender.
2. When that is ready, add the salt, dill, tahini, olive oil, and zucchini to the mix and blend.
3. When this is nice and smooth, you can pour the ingredients into a bowl and serve when ready.

Nutrition: Calories: 243 g Carbs: 4.6 g Protein: 3.9 g Fat: 23.2 g

40. No-Bake Energy Balls

Preparation Time: 5 minutes **Cooking Time:** 40 minutes **Servings:** 6

INGREDIENTS

- ¾ cup raspberries
- 10 dates
- 1 pinch of sea salt
- 1 cup walnuts
- cups shredded soft-jelly coconut meat

DIRECTIONS

1. Place all of the ingredients into a high-quality food processor. All components should be well mixed.
2. Make no-bake energy balls after soaking your hands in water to make them wet.
3. For twenty to thirty minutes, freeze the tray containing all the balls.

Nutrition: Calories: 1246 g Carbs: 48.2 g Protein: 19 g Fat: 108.5 g

41. Basil Avocado Pasta Salad

Preparation Time: 5 minutes **Cooking Time:** 10 minutes **Servings:** 6

INGREDIENTS

- 1 chopped avocado
- 4 cups cooked spelt-pasta
- 1 cup chopped fresh basil
- 1 tsp agave syrup
- 1 tsp lime juice
- ¼ cup olive oil
- Sea salt

DIRECTIONS

1. Place the cooked pasta in a large bowl.
2. Add avocado and basil.
3. Stir everything together completely.
4. Mix the juice, oil, lime, agave syrup, and sea salt in a small bowl.
5. Over the pasta, drizzle the mixture and toss to combine thoroughly.

Nutrition: Calories: 2402 g Carbs: 282.6 g Protein: 63.7 g Fat: 112.9 g

42. Stewed Okra

Preparation Time: 5 minutes **Cooking Time:** 30 minutes **Servings:** 6

INGREDIENTS

- 2 cups of fresh okra
- Sea salt, to taste
- 1 tbsp avocado oil
- ½ cup fresh spring water

DIRECTIONS

1. Okra should be cooked in a skillet with spring water for 10 minutes at a low simmer.
2. Add sea salt to your taste as desired.

Nutrition: Calories: 154 g Carbs: 3.5 g Protein: 1 g Fat: 15.1 g

43. Wakame Salad

Preparation Time: 5 minutes **Cooking Time:** 15 minutes **Servings:** 6

INGREDIENTS

- 2 cups Wakame stems
- 1 tsp sesame seeds
- 1 tsp agave syrup
- 1 tsp lime juice
- 1 tsp sesame oil
- 1 tsp ginger powder

DIRECTIONS

1. The wakame stems should first soak for 10 minutes. Then flush.
2. In a small bowl, combine the agave syrup, ginger, lime juice, and sesame oil. Completely combine.
3. Place the wakame in a serving bowl. The dressing is sprinkled over top. Sprinkle sesame seeds.

Nutrition: Calories: 214 g Carbs: 4.8 g Protein: 21.4 g Fat: 12.2 g

44. Plant-Based Chickpea Quinoa Burgers

Preparation Time: 5 minutes **Cooking Time:** 15 minutes **Servings:** 6

INGREDIENTS

- 1 ½ cup cooked chickpeas
- 1 tbsp raw homemade sesame "tahini" butter for each patty
- You can also use garbanzo beans
- Vegetables of your liking for serving
- 1 ½ cup cooked quinoa
- 2 tbsp fresh and recommended herbs of your liking
- 2 tbsp water
- ¼ cup cooked amaranth
- Sea salt, to taste
- You may use wild arugula, watercress, or lettuce

DIRECTIONS

1. The oven temperature is set at 375°F.
2. Put the herbs in a food processor. Pulse them until very finely chopped. Add the chickpeas, amaranth, and quinoa, and start the processor. You want the paste and purée to remain somewhat lumpy; do not mix them.
3. Add sea salt and continue mixing until a dough forms. Add water while the food processor is running to help the dough come together. You like the paste to be sticky rather than runny or dry. Place the bowl in the refrigerator to chill for half an hour.
4. After the mixture has cooled, divide it into eight equal-sized patties.
5. The patties should be baked for 20 minutes on a baking sheet coated with parchment paper. Flip the patties halfway through cooking and finish with a quick 2- to 3-minute broil to get the patties well browned.
6. Serve on an approved-flour bun with homemade "tahini" butter prepared from raw sesame seeds and wild arugula, lettuce, or watercress.

Nutrition: Calories: 991 g Carbs: 80.7 g Protein: 40.3 g Fat: 56.4 g

45. The Grilled Romaine Lettuce Salad

Preparation Time: 5 minutes   **Cooking Time:** 10 minutes   **Servings:** 6

INGREDIENTS

- 4 small heads of rinsed romaine lettuce
- 1 tsp agave syrup
- 1 tsp lime juice
- 4 tsp olive oil
- 1 tsp chopped fresh basil
- Sea salt, to your taste

DIRECTIONS

1. Put lettuce halves in a large nonstick dish, and cut side down. Use no oil at all.
2. Check the lettuce's color by turning it. Make sure to evenly brown all sides of the lettuce.
3. Place the lettuce on a large platter and turn off the heat in the pan.
4. Mix agave syrup, olive oil, lime juice, and fresh basil for the dressing in a small mixing bowl. Add salt for flavor. To properly blend, stir.
5. Sprinkle the dressing over the grilled lettuce after shifting it.

You need to make healthy food options your priority in order to avoid acid reflux issues and complications.

Nutrition: Calories: 676 g Carbs: 22.8 g Protein: 7.5 g Fat: 61.7 g

Chapter 3
First Course

46. Carrot-Ginger Salad

Preparation Time: 20 minutes
Stand: 15 minutes
Chill: 30 minutes
Servings: 10

INGREDIENTS

Salad:
- ½ cup slivered almonds
- ½ cup golden raisins
- ½ cup dried cranberries
- 1 lb carrots, shredded (about 5 medium carrots)

Dressing:
- ⅓ cup rice vinegar
- 2 tbsp freshly grated ginger
- 2 tbsp finely chopped cilantro
- 2 tsp salt
- 1 tsp sugar
- ½ cup canola oil

DIRECTIONS

1. **Make the salad:** Toast the almonds in a pan over medium heat. Cook, often stirring, for 7 to 10 minutes or until lightly golden. In a bowl, put it in a cool place. Allow the raisins and cranberries in a small bowl, cover with boiling water, and steep for 15 minutes. Drain. Toss with carrots in a large mixing bowl.
2. **Make the dressing:** Whisk together all of the ingredients in a small bowl. Toss the carrot mixture in the bowl to evenly coat the veggies with the dressing. Refrigerate for 30 minutes after covering. Toss in the almonds right before serving.

Nutrition: Calories: 1873 g Carbs: 125.8 g Protein: 24.2 g Fat: 141.2 g

47. Ginger Honeydew Soup

Preparation Time: 5 minutes **Cooking Time:** 1 hour **Servings:** 4

INGREDIENTS

- ½ cups honeydew melon
- 2 tbsp pure maple syrup
- 1 ½ to tsp grated fresh ginger
- cup plain yogurt (non-fat)
- 2 tsp crystallized ginger (finely minced)

DIRECTIONS

1. Combine the honeydew melon, maple syrup, and fresh ginger in a blender or food processor. One hour in the fridge is enough time for the mixture to thicken.
2. Swirl some yogurt into each plate and top with crystallized ginger.

Nutrition: Calories: 155 g Carbs: 30.4 g Protein: 7.9 g Fat: 0.2 g

48. Squash Soup

Preparation Time: 5 minutes **Cooking Time:** 30 minutes **Servings:** 6

INGREDIENTS

- ½ stick unsalted butter
- ½ medium sweet onion, diced (about 1 cup)
- 3 stalks of celery, chopped (about 1 cup)
- ⅓ cup flour
- 4 cups of vegetable broth
- 2 tsp herb blend (I use a fine herb blend or Savory Spice Shop Renaissance Blend)
- 1 tsp kosher salt
- 2 cups of red potato, diced (about six small potatoes)
- 4 cups butternut squash, chopped (about a tiny squash)
- 1 to 10 oz container of baby kale or kale/spinach blend
- 2 cups fat-free half and half

DIRECTIONS

1. Melt butter in a stockpot. Cook for 5 to 7 minutes or until onion and celery are soft.
2. Cook for 1 minute over medium heat after whisking in the flour. Cook, constantly stirring, until the soup has thickened.
3. Herbs, salt as needed.
4. We should add potato and butternut squash at this point—Cook for 20 minutes on low heat.
5. Cook for 2 minutes or until the kale has wilted. Reduce the volume to a minimum.
6. Mix the half-and-half and stir well. Bring to a boil, but not to a boil—season with salt.

Nutrition: Calories: 1134 g Carbs: 126.2 g Protein: 31.6 g Fat: 55.9 g

49. Flank Steak

Preparation Time: 10 minutes   **Cooking Time:** 20 minutes   **Servings:** 4

INGREDIENTS

- ¼ cup honey
- ¼ cup soy sauce
- ½ cup red wine
- A pinch of dried rosemary, crushed
- 1 lb flank steak

DIRECTIONS

1. Mix a bowl of red wine, honey, soy sauce, and rosemary.
2. Pour this marinade over the steak and let it marinate for 24 hours.
3. Preheat the grill over high heat and grease its grilling grate with oil.
4. Grill the steak for 7 minutes per side.
5. Serve.

Nutrition: Calories: 906 g Carbs: 47.4 g Protein: 104.3 g Fat: 25 g

50. Marinated Lamb Steaks

Preparation Time: 10 minutes   **Cooking Time:** 30 minutes   **Servings:** 6

INGREDIENTS

- 6 lamb leg steaks
- ½ cup dark coconut aminos
- 1 tbsp curry powder
- 1 tsp ground ginger
- 1 tbsp nonfat yogurt
- 1 tbsp olive oil
- 1 tbsp salt
- 2 cups new potatoes
- ⅔ cup pot natural yogurt
- 1 bunch of spring onions

DIRECTIONS

1. Combine everything for the marinade and rub it over the lamb steaks.
2. Let it marinate for 1 hour at room temperature.
3. Meanwhile, boil the potatoes in the salted water, drain them, and let them cool down.
4. Mix yogurt with spring onion and mint.
5. Toss in potatoes and seasonings.
6. Preheat the grill and grill the lamb steaks for 3 minutes per side.
7. Serve with potatoes mixture.

Nutrition: Calories: 2628 g Carbs: 59.4 g Protein: 203.7 g Fat: 175 g

51. Mediterranean Pizza

Preparation Time: 20 minutes **Servings:** 12 persons

INGREDIENTS

- 4 sliced basil leaves
- 1 crust, 2 pitas of readymade pizza dough
- 3 oz goat cheese, or ricotta
- 1 tbsp olive oil

DIRECTIONS

1. Set your oven's temperature to 450°F.
2. The pizza crust should be covered in olive oil.
3. Goat cheese should be placed on top of the basil and evenly spaced across the pizza.
4. According to the directions on the crust package, bake for 10 to 15 minutes in the oven.

Nutrition: Calories: 951 g Carbs: 119.1 g Protein: 26.1 g Fat: 41.2 g

52. Oven Blasted Vegetables

Preparation Time: 10 minutes **Cooking Time:** 15 minutes **Servings:** 4

INGREDIENTS

- ¾ cup carrots
- 1 Yukon gold potato
- 1 yam
- ¼ cup fruit vinegar
- 1 beet
- 1 tbsp cottage cheese
- 2 tbsp olive oil

DIRECTIONS

1. Cut vegetables into equal-sized pieces, either coin-shaped or lengthwise.
2. Oil in a flat metal pan needs to be heated for 2 minutes in a 500°F oven.
3. Add the cubed potatoes and carrots and cook for about 10 minutes.
4. Stirring every 10 minutes, continue cooking for a further 20 minutes after adding the beets and yam after another 5 minutes of cooking.
5. Remove from heat and serve with vinegar and cottage cheese for seasoning.

Nutrition: Calories: 600 g Carbs: 62.1 g Protein: 11.2 g Fat: 34.2 g

53. Irish Baked Potato Soup

Preparation Time: 10 minutes   **Cooking Time:** 30 minutes   **Servings:** 4

INGREDIENTS

- 4 oz cheese, cubed
- 2 large potatoes
- 4 cups skim milk
- 1/4 cup fat-free sour cream
- cup flour
- Salt, to taste

DIRECTIONS

1. Bake potatoes at 400°F until done.
2. Before slicing lengthwise and scooping out the pulp, let it cool.
3. Over a medium flame, toast the flour to a light brown color. Add the milk gradually while constantly stirring until thoroughly combined.
4. Add the potato pulp and salt to taste.
5. Cook over a medium flame, frequently stirring, until thick and bubbling.
6. The cheese should be well melted before adding it.
7. Stir in the sour cream after taking the pan off the heat.

Nutrition: Calories: 1224 g Carbs: 124.3 g Protein: 79.4 g Fat: 45.5 g

54. Vegan Mexican Cheese Pourable

Preparation Time: 5 minutes **Cooking Time:** 5 minutes **Servings:** 8

INGREDIENTS

- ¾ cup (108g) raw cashews (See observation)
- ¾ cup (180g) salsa (I used Trader Joe's medium heat, this makes it spicy, if you don't want it too spicy, use a mild salsa)
- ¾ cup (180g) water
- 6 tbsp (36g) nutritional yeast (I highly recommend this Sari brand, it is non-fortified with a much better taste)
- 2 to 3 tsp ground cumin (to preferred taste)
- ½ tsp + tsp salt

DIRECTIONS

1. Pre-soak cashews in a Vitamix blender. Drain and rinse the cashews after soaking for 8 hours.
2. In a blender, mix all of the ingredients and blend until smooth and creamy. Taste and season with additional salt if necessary. Based on the acidity of my salsa, I found the amount to be precisely correct, but you may need to modify it.
3. In a small saucepan, mix the sauce and reduce the heat to low. Allow it to simmer for about 5 minutes or until it has thickened somewhat. It will thicken as time goes on. To keep it from sticking too much, whisk it down the sides now and again. It's best not to walk away from it while it's cooking since it cooks rapidly. If it sticks a bit, don't worry; you can always smooth it out. It's essential to cook it on low heat because the cheese will thicken and get crusty if you cook it on high. It should just take around 5 minutes. It will take a little longer for the tahini version to thicken. After cooking, the color will deepen somewhat to a more genuine cheesy hue. Pour into a serving bowl and whisk well to smooth out. If serving as a dip, drizzle additional salsa on top. If yours is light, it's a good idea to put a bit of extra salsa on top to keep it from being too spicy. Serve immediately with tacos, burritos, and other meals.
4. Refrigerate any leftovers. If it thickens in the fridge, you can whisk it and thin it with water, but it will stay creamy and smooth. Reheat slowly.

Nutrition: Calories: 1486 g Carbs: 96.7 g Protein: 85.4 g Fat: 84.3 g

55. Crispy Oven-Baked Chicken Tenders

Preparation Time: 10 minutes   **Cooking Time:** 25 minutes   **Servings:** 4

INGREDIENTS

- 1 ½ cup panko breadcrumbs (see note one)
- Oil spray
- 1 tbsp butter
- 1 egg
- 1 tbsp mayonnaise
- 1 and ½ tbsp Dijon mustard (or other mustard)
- 2 tbsp flour
- ½ tsp salt
- 500 g/ 1 lb chicken tenderloins (or breast cut into 2/3" / 1.5cm thick slices, lengthwise)
- Oil spray

Crumbing:

6. Pick up the chicken with tongs and put it in the panko dish.
7. Breadcrumbs need to be spread out and pushed down to stick to the surface. Set in a baking pan. Repeat with the leftover chicken; clean fingers are amazing.
8. Spray with a little oil and salt before cooking (optional). Bake for 15 minutes for medium or 20 minutes for huge in the oven. The chicken will be dried out if you wait much longer.
9. Take the food out of the oven and serve it immediately with your favorite sauce (honey mustard is shown in the photo; see note 2 for more information), if you'd like, and fresh parsley.

DIRECTIONS

1. The oven should be preheated to 390°F (200°C).
2. On a baking sheet, spray panko and bake for 3 to 5 minutes or until lightly golden (spray vertically to avoid blowing the panko off the surface). Transfer the mixture to a bowl.
3. Place a rack on an oven rack (not critical, but it bakes more evenly).
4. Combine the batter ingredients in a mixing basin with a fork and whisk until combined.
5. Completely coat the chicken with the batter by tossing it.

Nutrition: Calories: 1938 g Carbs: 143.8 g Protein: 128.1 g Fat: 94.6 g

56. Roast Rib of Beef

Preparation Time: 10 minutes **Cooking Time:** 45 minutes **Servings:** 6

INGREDIENTS

- 2 Knorr beef stock cubes
- 1 tbsp olive oil
- 3 lb rib of beef
- 5 small leeks
- 6 parsnips, peeled and halved
- 6 carrots, peeled and halved
- 4 shallots, peeled and halved
- 2 Celery sticks cut into large chunks
- 1 tbsp fresh sage leaves

DIRECTIONS

1. Set the oven to 400°F.
2. Mix 1 Knorr beef cube with 1 tbsp of oil and rub this paste onto the beef.
3. Sear the beef in a greased pan until brown, then transfer them to a roasting pan.
4. Sauté leeks in the same pan until golden and place them around the beef.
5. Now sauté carrots and parsnips in the pan and transfer them to the roasting pan.
6. Top the beef with sage, celery, and shallots.
7. Bake for 45 minutes. Serve.

Nutrition: Calories: 2351 g Carbs: 143.4 g Protein: 308.1 g Fat: 60.6 g

57. Rosemary Broiled Shrimp

Preparation Time: 10 minutes **Cooking Time:** 4 minutes **Servings:** 2

INGREDIENTS

- ¾ lb large shrimps, shelled and deveined
- 1 tsp extra virgin olive oil
- 1 tbsp Himalayan crystal salt, to taste
- ½ tsp dried rosemary, crushed

DIRECTIONS

1. Preheat the broiler and place the rack 4 inches from the heat. Line a baking tray with foil.
2. Place the shrimp on the prepared baking tray in a single layer. Drizzle with the oil. With the rosemary and salt, sprinkle over the shrimp.
3. Broil for about 3 to 4 minutes. Remove from the heat and serve.

Nutrition: Calories: 392 g Carbs: 11.8 g Protein: 46.4 g Fat: 17.6 g

58. Turkey Stew

Preparation Time: 15 minutes **Cooking Time:** 22 minutes **Servings:** 2

INGREDIENTS

- 1 tsp extra virgin olive oil
- 1 celery stalk, minced
- ¼ tsp freshly ground coriander
- ½ tsp freshly ground cumin
- ½ lb lean ground turkey
- ½ cup low-sodium vegetable broth
- 1 tbsp Himalayan crystal salt, to taste

DIRECTIONS

1. In a pan, heat the oil on medium heat; add the celery and sauté for 4 minutes.
2. Add the coriander and cumin, and sauté for a further minute.
3. Add the turkey and cook, stirring, for 6 to 7 minutes. Add the remaining ingredients. Increase the heat and bring the pan to a boil. Once boiling, cover and simmer for about 8 to 10 minutes.

Nutrition: Calories: 414 g Carbs: 2.2 g Protein: 51.8 g Fat: 22.1 g

59. Oat and Chickpea Dumplings

Preparation Time: 5 minutes **Cooking Time:** 15 minutes **Servings:** 4

INGREDIENTS

- 6 tbsp rapeseed oil
- 2 medium onions, finely chopped
- 2 tsp ground cumin
- 2 cans of chickpeas, drained
- 1 pack coriander
- ½ cup oats

DIRECTIONS

1. Grease a frying pan with 2 tbsp of oil and sauté onions for 5 minutes until golden.
2. Stir in cumin and cook for 1 minute, then keep the mixture in a food processor.
3. Add coriander, chickpeas, seasoning, and 2 tbsp of oil. Blend until smooth.
4. Fold in oats and make 16 small balls from it.
5. Heat oil for frying and cook the dumpling for 3 minutes.
6. Stir in passata along with water and let it simmer for 2 minutes.
7. Serve warm.

Nutrition: Calories: 1653 g Carbs: 125.6 g Protein: 45.8 g Fat: 107.5 g

60. Lamb Kofta Curry

Preparation Time: 10 minutes **Cooking Time:** 50 minutes **Servings:** 4

INGREDIENTS

- 2 tbsp olive oil
- 2 red onions, finely chopped
- 5 cm piece root ginger, grated
- 2 tsp ground cumin
- 1 tsp turmeric
- 1 tsp ground coriander
- 2 cups minced lamb
- ½ cup fine fresh white breadcrumbs
- 2 tbsp chopped coriander
- 1 egg beaten
- 2 tsp Panch Phoron seasoning
- 2 cups non-fat yogurt
- 1 cup hot vegetable stock
- 2 bay leaves
- 4 tbsp coconut cream

DIRECTIONS

1. Preheat the grill to medium heat.
2. Heat oil in a suitable frying pan, sauté ginger, and onions for 5 minutes.
3. Reserve half this mixture and add turmeric, coriander ground, and cumin.
4. Cook for 1 minute, then remove it from the heat.
5. Mix minced meat with coriander, egg, and breadcrumbs.
6. Toss in onion mix and make small balls from this mixture.
7. Arrange the lamb meatballs in the baking dish and grill for 15 minutes.
8. Make the sauce by mixing onion mixture of oriental spices. Cook for 2 minutes.
9. Add yogurt, stock, seasoning, and bay leaves. Cook for 15 minutes.
10. Discard the bay leaves and stir in coconut cream.
11. Blend the mixture, then add meatballs. Cook for 10 minutes.
12. Serve.

Nutrition: Calories: 1836 g Carbs: 100.2 g Protein: 124.7 g Fat: 104.1 g

61. Vegetarian Pasta Bakes With Halloumi

Preparation Time: 10 minutes **Cooking Time:** 40 minutes **Servings:** 4

INGREDIENTS

- 2 cups conchiglie pasta
- 2 cups frozen broad beans
- ⅔ cup mascarpone
- ¼ cup pack of watercress
- 2 x 1 cup packs of chargrilled artichokes, thinly sliced
- 1 ⅓ cup halloumi, cubed
- 1 large red chili, sliced (optional)

DIRECTIONS

1. Set the oven to 400°F. Meanwhile, boil salted water in a pan.
2. Add pasta to the water and cook for 10 minutes. Stir in broad beans.
3. Cook for 2 minutes, then adds mascarpone.
4. Chop watercress and add it to the pasta
5. Spread half of the pasta mixture in a baking dish and top it with sliced artichokes.
6. Add the remaining half of the pasta. Top it with halloumi cubes.
7. Bake for 30 minutes.
8. Garnish as desired and serve.

Nutrition: Calories: 2048 g Carbs: 248.5 g Protein: 70.9 g Fat: 85.7 g

62. Beetroot and Carrots

Preparation Time: 5 minutes **Cooking Time:** 30 minutes **Servings:** 4

INGREDIENTS

- 4 medium carrots, diced
- 1 tbsp balsamic vinegar
- 2 tbsp clear honey
- 1 tbsp olive oil
- 4 pre-cooked beets (not in vinegar), quartered
- 25g pumpkin seeds
- A handful of fresh herbs (parsley or basil) to serve

DIRECTIONS

1. Preheat oven to 356°F/320°F fan/gas 4 (180°C/160°C fan/gas 4). Toss the carrots, vinegar, honey, and olive oil in a mixing bowl. Roast for 30 minutes after spreading on a baking pan.
2. Remove the tray from the oven 5 minutes before the end of the cooking time, add the beetroot, and return it to the oven. Remove from the oven once ready and cool slightly before tossing with the pumpkin seeds and herbs.

Nutrition: Calories: 506 g Carbs: 72.2 g Protein: 9.2 g Fat: 20 g

63. Ginger Snap Beef Stew

Preparation Time: 8 minutes
Cooking Time: 7 hours
Marinating time: 12 hours
Servings: 4

INGREDIENTS

- 2 ¼ lb cubed sirloin
- ¾-1 cup red wine vinegar
- 1 large onion, sliced into half-moons
- 2 carrots, cut into ½-inch chunks
- 2 bay leaves
- ½ tsp ground allspice
- ¾ tsp ground mustard
- ¼ tsp cloves
- ¼ tsp salt
- 1 ¼ lb Russet potatoes, cubed
- 10 gingersnaps, broken into pieces

DIRECTIONS

1. Combine all of the ingredients from the first step in a big ziplock bag and marinate overnight. If you're utilizing handmade gingersnaps, now is an excellent time to make them.
2. In a 4-quart slow cooker, place the potatoes. Add the beef mixture that has been marinated. We should sprinkle gingersnaps on top—Cook for 7 hours on low. Remove the bay leaves from the meal. If feasible, stir once during the day and just before serving.

In order to prevent acid reflux, we need to get help from food!

Nutrition: Calories: 1750 g Carbs: 272.6 g Protein: 80.4 g Fat: 37.4 g

Chapter 4
Main Course

64. Creamy Herb Mushroom Chicken

Preparation Time: 10 minutes **Cooking Time:** 15 minutes **Servings:** 4

INGREDIENTS

- ½ lb mushrooms, rinsed and patted dry
- 1 lb chicken tenders
- 1 tbsp butter, divided
- 1 tbsp olive oil, divided
- ¼ cup chopped fresh dill
- ¼ cup chopped fresh parsley
- ¼ cup chopped green onion
- ¾ cup heavy whipping cream

DIRECTIONS

1. Herbs and mushrooms should be minced, chopped, and sliced.
2. Cook over medium heat with ½ tsp butter and ½ tsp oil. Once the oil is heated, add the mushrooms and salt and cook for a few minutes. Remove to a platter after 5 minutes of cooking, during which time you should toss the mushrooms regularly until they are golden brown.
3. 1 tsp of salt may be used to season the chicken all over. Add another ½ tbsp of butter and ½ tbsp of oil to the same pan over medium heat. Simmer for approximately 2 minutes on each side or until the chicken is just cooked through.
4. To soften the herbs, add them to the pan with the dill, parsley, and green onion and cook/stir for an additional minute.
5. Return the mushrooms to the pan, then add ¾ cup of heavy cream and stir. 2 minutes more at a simmer or until the sauce has thickened slightly before turning off the heat. Slowly, the sauce will get thicker as it cools down.

Nutrition: Calories: 1770 g Carbs: 94.9 g Protein: 126.1 g Fat: 98.6 g

65. Steak With Onion

Preparation Time: 10 minutes **Cooking Time:** 25 minutes **Servings:** 4

INGREDIENTS

- 4 tsp butter
- 2 medium onions, sliced
- 1 tbsp brown sugar
- tsp salt
- 1 lb boneless beef top sirloin steak, trimmed of fat
- 1 tbsp balsamic vinegar
- 1 tbsp snipped fresh parsley

DIRECTIONS

1. In a medium pan, melt the butter over low heat.
2. Toss in the onions
3. Cook for 13 to 15 minutes, wrapped, or until onions are tender.
4. Mix the brown sugar and salt in a mixing bowl.
5. Cook, constantly stirring, for 4 to 5 minutes over medium-high heat or until onions are golden brown.
6. Cut the meat into four serving-size pieces in the meantime.
7. Season both sides of every meat piece with salt.
8. Place on a broiler pan's unheated shelf.
9. Broil 3 inches away from the heat before finishing to your liking, turning once.
10. (For medium rare, allow 10 to 12 minutes.) Toss the onions with vinegar.
11. Place the onion mixture on top of the steak.
12. Serve with a parsley garnish.

Nutrition: Calories: 1186 g Carbs: 32.2 g Protein: 106.7 g Fat: 70 g

66. Lamb Stew With Olives

Preparation Time: 10 minutes **Cooking Time:** 1 hour 20 minutes **Servings:** 4

INGREDIENTS

- 2 tbsp olive oil
- 500g lamb neck fillet, cubed
- 1 onion, sliced
- 125ml dry white wine
- 2 x 5cm strips of orange peel (pith removed)
- 2 sprigs thyme
- A handful of pitted Kalamata olives
- Crusty bread, to serve

DIRECTIONS

1. In a large skillet or pan, heat one tbsp of olive oil. Cook for 5 to 10 minutes or until the lamb is browned all over. Remove the pan from the heat and set it aside.
2. Heat the remaining oil in the same pan, add the onion, and simmer for 5 minutes or soften. Cook for another 31 seconds
3. Turn up the heat and add the white wine. Bring to a boil, then simmer for 2 to 3 minutes or until the liquid has been reduced by half.
4. Return the lamb, orange peel, thyme sprigs, and 200ml water to the pan. Allow to simmer for 1 hour, adding a splash of water if necessary.
5. Cook for another 20 minutes before adding olives. Remove the orange peel before serving, and serve with crusty bread if desired.

Nutrition: Calories: 1808 g Carbs: 75.6 g Protein: 103.4 g Fat: 111.6 g

67. Sweet and Crunchy Coleslaw

Preparation Time: 10 minutes **Cooking Time:** 30 minutes **Servings:** 4

INGREDIENTS

- 1 tsp celery seed
- 6 cups shredded cabbage
- ½ cup rice vinegar
- 1 cup sugar
- 1 onion
- ¼ cups tofu, cut into 2cm (1in) cubes
- 1 tsp yellow prepared mustard
- 1/4 cup canola oil

DIRECTIONS

1. Shredded cabbage should be placed inside a sizable mixing bowl.
2. Blend the remaining ingredients until completely smooth.
3. The onion and cabbage should be covered in dressing. After thoroughly combining, refrigerate.
4. Cool completely before serving.

Nutrition: Calories: 1506 g Carbs: 231.6 g Protein: 18.6 g Fat: 56.2 g

68. Mediterranean Green Beans

Preparation Time: 10 minutes   **Cooking Time:** 15 minutes   **Servings:** 4

INGREDIENTS

- 2 ½ tsp olive oil
- 1 lb green beans fresh, trimmed to 1- to 2-inch pieces
- ¾ cup water

DIRECTIONS

1. Bring water to a boil in a sizable nonstick skillet. Add the beans and cook for about 3 minutes. Set aside after draining.
2. Add the beans to a skillet over medium-high heat and cook for 1 minute.
3. After adding the juice, cook for an additional minute.

Nutrition: Calories: 220 g Carbs: 10.8 g Protein: 9.5 g Fat: 15.5 g

69. Summer Vegetable Kebabs

Preparation Time: 10 minutes   **Cooking Time:** 20 minutes   **Servings:** 4

INGREDIENTS

- 2 tbsp olive oil
- 1 tbsp peach jam
- 1 tsp Mrs. Dash herb seasoning blend
- 1 medium zucchini
- 1 medium yellow summer squash
- ¼ tsp salt

DIRECTIONS

1. Liquefy the peach jam in a small microwave-safe bowl for 10 to 15 seconds to create the marinade. Combine the Mrs. Dash herb seasoning, olive oil, and salt in a large mixing bowl. Stir everything together thoroughly.
2. Cut the vegetables into uniform bite-sized pieces for the kebabs. Combine them with the saved marinade in a medium mixing bowl. Add the sauce to the vegetables and toss to coat.
3. Thread the vegetables on skewers.
4. Set your grill's temperature to medium-high. The skewers should be cooked on the grill and covered for 12 to 15 minutes. Turn the skewers 2 or 3 times to ensure even cooking.

Nutrition: Calories: 456 g Carbs: 32.8 g Protein: 12 g Fat: 30.7 g

70. Baked Potato Soup

Preparation Time: 10 minutes   **Cooking Time:** 25 minutes   **Servings:** 4

INGREDIENTS

- ½ cup fat-free sour cream
- 2 large potatoes
- 4 oz shredded low-fat Monterey jack cheese
- cup flour
- 4 cups skim milk

DIRECTIONS

1. Bake potatoes at 400°F until fork-tender. Let it cool.
2. Make a lengthwise cut. Then remove the pulp with a spoon.
3. You should put flour in a large saucepan. Then, while stirring, gradually add the milk. Next, potato pulp is added.
4. Cook, frequently stirring, over a medium flame until thick and bubbling.
5. Once the cheese has been added, it should be stirred until it melts. Eject from the flame.
6. Finally, stir in the sour cream.

Nutrition: Calories: 1109 g Carbs: 130.6 g Protein: 54.3 g Fat: 41.2 g

71. Grilled Vegetable Pasta Salad

Preparation Time: 10 minutes   **Cooking Time:** 20 minutes   **Servings:** 4

INGREDIENTS

- 1 tbsp chopped fresh parsley
- 2 tbsp fresh basil leaves, shredded
- 2 medium sliced zucchini
- 12 oz rotini, uncooked
- 1 head of anise (fennel), sliced
- 1 tbsp and 1 tsp Dijon mustard
- 8 mushrooms, quartered
- ¼ cup olive oil
- 1 tbsp fresh thyme

DIRECTIONS

1. In a large mixing bowl, combine all of the veggies. After that, pour half of the dressing over the veggies and mix to evenly cover everything. While the pasta is being cooked in accordance with the directions on the box, let the veggies marinade. Cold water should be used to rinse pasta.
2. Turn on the broiler setting in the oven. If using the oven, use a buttered broiler pan.
3. The vegetables must then be spread out on a broiling pan and roasted until golden brown. To ensure consistent browning, the food should be stirred every 4 to 5 minutes. Once browned, transfer to a large serving bowl. Fresh herbs, leftover dressing, and pasta should be included.

Nutrition: Calories: 1864 g Carbs: 296.4 g Protein: 50.6 g Fat: 52.9 g

72. Miso-Glazed Scallops

Preparation Time: 10 minutes   **Cooking Time:** 15 minutes   **Servings:** 4

INGREDIENTS

- 2 tbsp white miso (I used a darker miso since I didn't disclose that I did, but I also have the freedom to do it.)
- 3 tbsp mirin, divided
- 3 tbsp sake, divided (seasoned rice vinegar also works)
- 2 tbsp sugar, divided
- 1 lb scallops (dry is ideal, but wet will work just fine, especially with the sugar-crust method here)
- 2 tsp olive oil
- 2 to 3 tbsp sliced scallions (about 1 scallion)

DIRECTIONS

1. Refrigerate the scallops overnight in order to thaw them. Place the scallops in a covered container lined with paper towels. Alternatively, you might immerse the package in cold water for 30 minutes before letting it air dry. When the scallops have thawed, dry them off and put them on a dish lined with paper towels.
2. In a medium bowl large enough to hold the scallops, whisk the miso, 2 tsp mirin, 2 tbsp sake, and 1 tbsp sugar. Scallops should marinate for 10 to 15 minutes after being added.
3. Put the remaining sugar in a little shallow dish and add the scallops once they have marinated. Every scallop should be taken out of the miso marinade and shaken to get as much of the marinade off as possible. The scallop should then be dipped on one side of the sugar and placed on the same plate as previously. Save the marinade to use later to create a sauce.
4. Heat the oil over medium-high heat in a large frypan for 1 to 2 minutes or until it sizzles hot. Put a single layer of scallops on the pan with the sugar side facing up. Give it 2 minutes to cool without touching it. The bottoms have to be well-browned and caramelized. Use a fish spatula to loosen and rotate each scallop. Extract to a dish after cooking for a further 1 to 2 minutes.
5. Add the remaining 1 tbsp mirin, 1 tbsp sake, and the marinade in a different pan. Cook for 30 to 60 seconds, scraping out any brown bits from the scallops, or until the sauce starts to turn a light shade darker. Serve immediately after pouring over the scallops and adding sliced scallions as a garnish.

Nutrition: Calories: 763 g Carbs: 54.9 g Protein: 59.1 g Fat: 34.2 g

73. Mashed Cauliflower Potatoes

Preparation Time: 10 minutes **Cooking Time:** 25 minutes **Servings:** 4

INGREDIENTS

- 1 medium red potato
- 1 tsp dried parsley
- 8 oz cauliflower florets
- 2 tbsp margarine

DIRECTIONS

1. In a medium saucepan, combine the potato, parsley, and cauliflower. Add just enough water to cover the ingredients.
2. High heat should be used to bring it to a boil, and then the flame should be lowered to a simmer.
3. Vegetables should be cooked for 12 minutes or until soft and properly drained.
4. Use a potato masher to mash the potatoes.
5. Add the margarine and mash it until smooth.

Nutrition: Calories: 462 g Carbs: 42.2 g Protein: 11.8 g Fat: 27.4 g

74. Zucchini and Carrots Frittata

Preparation Time: 10 minutes **Cooking Time:** 22 minutes **Servings:** 4

INGREDIENTS

- 4 eggs
- ½ cup grated carrot
- ½ cup grated zucchini
- ¼ cup shredded mozzarella cheese
- Scant ¼ cup chopped parsley, loosely packed
- Salt
- Optional extras: Grated parmesan cheese, extra mozzarella, or pine nuts

DIRECTIONS

1. Preheat the oven to 350°F. We should grease a muffin pan with five holes. First, make sure the muffin holes are correctly greased.
2. In a large mixing bowl, mix the eggs using a fork. Next, mix the carrots, zucchini, mozzarella cheese, parsley, and salt in a large mixing bowl. Mix until everything is well mixed. We should mix optional add-ins in now.
3. Fill the muffin skillet or pan with the mixture and place it in the five holes that have been made. Preheat oven to 180°F and bake for 18 to 22 minutes or until set. Allow the frittatas to cool in the pan for 5 minutes before removing them. Enjoy!

Nutrition: Calories: 446 g Carbs: 7 g Protein: 39.2 g Fat: 29.1 g

75. Steamer Clams With Bacon and Fennel

Preparation Time: 10 minutes **Cooking Time:** 10 minutes **Servings:** 4

INGREDIENTS

- 2 lb fresh steamer clams littleneck / Manila clams, scrubbed clean
- 3 tbsp olive oil
- ½ shallot minced

Grilled toast:

- 4 slices rustic french bread cut into 1-inch thick slices
- 1 to 2 tbsp butter
- 1 cup white wine such as pinot grigio (mild white wine)
- 6 slices bacon cut in lardons
- ½ shallot, sliced
- 1 to 2 tbsp fresh fennel off the stem

DIRECTIONS

1. Render the bacon lardon's fat in a large pan over moderate heat (cook slowly enough to cook the fat out and not burn the bacon). The bacon should be placed on a paper towel to absorb any additional oil. Shallot slices should be sautéed in the bacon oil for approximately a minute or until just softened. Extract to a bowl, then stir in the bacon.
2. Heat the food at a medium-high level. Olive oil should be added to the pan. Minced shallots and clams should be added. The clams should be cooked for around 2 minutes with constant stirring. 1 tbsp fresh fennel and a little wine. Cook until the clams have opened while covered.
3. Take the pan off the stove. To the pan, add the bacon-onion combination. Serve with grilled bread.

Nutrition: Calories: 1400 g Carbs: 23.6 g Protein: 104.1 g Fat: 83 g

76. Thai Tofu and Red Cabbage Bowl

Preparation Time: 10 minutes **Cooking Time:** 40 minutes **Servings:** 4

INGREDIENTS

For the tofu:

- 2 tbsp groundnut oil
- 2 tbsp lemon grass
- 3 ¼ cups tofu, cut into 2cm (1in) cubes
- 1 red bird's-eye chili, finely sliced
- cup (1 ½ oz) pieces of ginger, sliced
- 4 spring onions, sliced
- 1 lime, juiced
- 2 tbsp coconut amino
- ½ small red cabbage, sliced
- ½ cup (3 ½ oz) snap peas
- 2 tbsp (½ oz) basil leaves, sliced
- 4 tbsp peanuts, toasted and roughly chopped, to serve
- 1 lime, quartered, to serve
- 2 cups (10 oz) easy cook brown rice

DIRECTIONS

1. Add rice, lemon grass, and 1 pt. water to a cooking pot.
2. Boil the rice, then reduce the heat to cook for 25 minutes until al dente.
3. Meanwhile, heat oil in a wok and sauté tofu for 6 minutes.
4. Add spring onion, ginger, and chili. Stir and cook for 1 minute.
5. Add coconut amino and lime juice.
6. Stir in snap peas and red cabbage. Cook for 3 minutes.
7. Add basil, then put off the heat.
8. To serve, add rice to the serving bowl and then top them with the tofu mixture.
9. Garnish with peanuts. Serve.

Nutrition: Calories: 1917 g Carbs: 253.2 g Protein: 55.2 g Fat: 76 g

77. Mushroom Chicken and Rice

Preparation Time: 15 minutes   **Cooking Time:** 1 hour   **Servings:** 6

INGREDIENTS

- 2 tsp olive oil
- 6-8 bone-in, skin-on, chicken thighs
- 6-8 medium button mushrooms, sliced
- 1 medium onion, diced
- 1 tbsp dried parsley
- 1 tsp dried thyme
- ½ tsp salt
- 2 cups low-sodium chicken broth
- ¼ cup heavy cream
- 1 cup long-grain white rice

DIRECTIONS

1. Preheat oven to 350°F.
2. Warm the olive oil in a covered oven-safe pan over medium heat.
3. Salt the chicken thighs and put them in the pan. Brown the chicken for 4 minutes; the chicken will not be cooked.
4. Discard the chicken and most of the fat, leaving 1 tsp or 2.
5. Stir in the mushrooms, and onions, and simmer for 4 to 5 minutes until softened.
6. Stir in parsley, thyme, and salt
7. Stir in chicken broth, cream, and rice. Simmer the liquid (steaming with small bubbles forming along the edges of the pot, but not quite boiling).
8. Cover the skillet with the chicken and the rice.
9. Bake for 35 minutes in a preheated oven. Remove the lid and bake for 10 minutes longer until the rice is soft.

Nutrition: Calories: 3139 g Carbs: 151.9 g Protein: 373.5 g Fat: 115.2 g

78. Baked Chicken Thighs

Preparation Time: 5 minutes   **Cooking Time:** 35 minutes   **Servings:** 8

INGREDIENTS

- 3 lb chicken thighs, about 6 to 8
- 2 tbsp olive oil
- 2 tsp salt
- 2 tsp onion powder
- 2 tsp Italian seasoning
- 1 tsp paprika

DIRECTIONS

1. After taking the chicken thighs from the packaging, pat them dry using paper towels. The chicken thighs should be placed on a baking pan and brushed with olive oil to coat them.
2. Mix the salt, onion powder, Italian spice and paprika in a small bowl. Evenly distribute the seasonings over the chicken.
3. In a preheated oven, cook the chicken for 35 to 45 minutes per pound.
4. Increase the cooking time or until the rice is done.

Nutrition: Calories: 1931 g Carbs: 24.1 g Protein: 245.1 g Fat: 94.9 g

79. Chicken Stew

Preparation Time: 15 minutes **Cooking Time:** 40 minutes **Servings:** 6

INGREDIENTS

- 8 chicken thighs about 1 ½ lb, diced
- 2 tsp olive oil
- 2 carrots diced
- 1 small onion
- 2 stalks celery diced
- 5 tbsp flour divided
- ½ tsp rosemary
- ½ tsp thyme
- ¼ tsp sage
- 1 tbsp salt
- 1 ½ cup potatoes peeled and diced
- 1 ½ cup sweet potatoes peeled and diced
- ¼ cup white wine
- 4 cups chicken broth
- 1 cup green beans or peas
- ½ cup heavy cream

DIRECTIONS

1. Brown the chicken in 1 tbsp of olive oil in a large saucepan. Take it out of the pot and place it in a safe place.
2. Stir-fry the remaining vegetables for 3 minutes or until the onion is softened. 3 tbsp of flour are added to the mixture, along with salt to taste—Cook for 2 minutes at medium heat.
3. Pour in white wine, browned chicken, and a cup of chicken broth. 30 minutes of simmering in the covered pot at a low heat
4. Then, remove the top, add green beans and heavy cream. Simmer for another 10 minutes, uncovered, to thicken if desired.
5. Mix the remaining 2 tbsp of flour with 1 cup of water or broth in a mason jar to thicken. Be careful to thoroughly shake the ingredients (to avoid any lumps) before adding to the simmering stew in small amounts until the required consistency is achieved.

Nutrition: Calories: 2648 g Carbs: 96.7 g Protein: 306.3 g Fat: 110.3 g

80. Edamame Stir Fry

Preparation Time: 5 minutes **Cooking Time:** 30 minutes **Servings:** 6

INGREDIENTS

- 1 cup rice brown rice
- 1 ½ cup vegetable broth
- ½ cup low-sodium soy sauce
- 1 tbsp cornstarch
- 1 tbsp peanut oil
- 3 cups frozen shelled edamame thawed
- 2 cups asparagus cut into ½ inch pieces
- 1-inch ginger root grated
- ½ cup cashews roasted and unsalted
- 1 cup green onions chopped

DIRECTIONS

1. Make the rice in a large pot according to the package directions.
2. Whisk together the broth, soy sauce, and cornstarch in a large measuring cup.
3. Preheat a large non-stick skillet over high heat with the peanut oil in it. Add edamame, asparagus, cashews and ginger once the oil is shimmering. Cook for 3 minutes until the bell pepper has softened and the asparagus is cooked but still crisp, stirring often.
4. Add broth and soy sauce to a small pan and heat to a low boil. Reduce the heat to medium-low and simmer, often stirring, for 3 minutes or until the sauce thickens. Stir in the green onions until everything is well mixed.
5. Serve the stir-fry with rice and more green onion, if preferred.

Nutrition: Calories: 1625 g Carbs: 219.8 g Protein: 82.7 g Fat: 46 g

81. Ham and Asparagus Quiche Bites

Preparation Time: 5 minutes **Cooking Time:** 30 minutes **Servings:** 6

INGREDIENTS

- 1 cup chopped asparagus
- 6 large eggs
- ¼ cup heavy whipping cream
- ½ tsp salt
- 1 cup grated swiss cheese
- ½ cup diced ham

DIRECTIONS

1. Preheat the oven to 350°F. Using a non-stick spray, spray a muffin pan.
2. In a small bowl, add the asparagus and 1 tbsp of water—microwave for 2 minutes, and carefully wrapped in plastic. Allow for a 2-minute cooling period before gently removing the plastic wrap. Remove the water from the bowl.
3. In a medium-sized mixing bowl, whisk eggs, cream, and salt jointly until thoroughly mixed.
4. In a mixing bowl, stir the asparagus, cheese, and ham.
5. Pour the mixture evenly into 8 muffin tins, ensuring the asparagus, ham, and cheese are correctly distributed.
6. Bake it for about 20 minutes, or until the eggs are set and the sides of the muffin pan are starting to peel away.
7. Allow cooling for 5 minutes before removing the muffins with a knife along the edges.
8. As desired, serve warm or cold.

Nutrition: Calories: 1597 g Carbs: 5.9 g Protein: 87.5 g Fat: 136 g

82. Baked Chicken Meatballs

Preparation Time: 5 minutes **Cooking Time:** 30 minutes **Servings:** 6

INGREDIENTS

- 1 lb ground chicken or turkey
- 1 egg
- ½ cup panko breadcrumbs
- ½ cup grated parmesan
- 2 tbsp olive oil
- ½ tsp onion powder
- ½ tsp salt

DIRECTIONS

1. Set the oven to 400°F. Cooking spray and foil a baking sheet.
2. Combine all items in a mixing bowl.
3. To roll, form the mixture into 30 little balls by rolling it between your hands on a baking sheet; place.
4. Bake for 25 to 30 minutes of baking time.
5. Enjoy!

If you want to treat acid reflux during the initial stage, trying these recipes will help.

Nutrition: Calories: 1671 g Carbs: 94.4 g Protein: 125 g Fat: 88.3 g

Chapter 5

Healthy and Tasty Recipes to Enjoy Life With Your Family and Your Friends

Don't give up on your social life!

You can manage meals when you are with family and friends, without sacrificing taste and conviviality. You can prepare these healthy and tasty meals when you have guests and still manage the symptoms of your acid reflux.

Tasty Sunday Lunch

83. Mushroom Rice

Preparation Time: 5 minutes　　**Cooking Time:** 30 minutes　　**Servings:** 6

INGREDIENTS

- 1 cup jasmine rice
- 1 can condensed mushroom soup
- 1 can of mushrooms undrained
- 1 ¾ cup water

DIRECTIONS

1. Bring one and a quarter cups of water to a boil. When the water begins to boil, cover it and lower the heat. For about 9 minutes, simmer. Use tongs or a fork to fluff the rice after it has cooked for approximately 2 minutes.
2. Mix the mushroom soup and the mushroom can. After combining, reheat to the desired temperature. Serve immediately.

Nutrition: Calories: 971 g Carbs: 168.7 g Protein: 27 g Fat: 21 g

84. Bananas Brulee with Vanilla Cream

Preparation Time: 15 minutes **Cooking Time:** 5 minutes **Servings:** 4

INGREDIENTS

Bananas Brulee:
- 4 medium-ripe bananas peeled and halved lengthwise
- ¼ cup coconut sugar

Vanilla bean cream:
- ½ cup coconut cream
- 2 tsp maple syrup
- ½ tsp vanilla/vanilla bean paste

DIRECTIONS

Bananas Brulee:
1. Place cut-side-up banana halves on a heat-proof baking sheet.
2. Sprinkle the coconut sugar on top, making sure it's fully covered.
3. Heat the sugar with a cooking torch until it is "burnt" or caramelized. Allow time for the sugar to solidify.
4. Alternately, place under the broiler on high in the oven until the sugar caramelizes. Keep an eye on the sugar to make sure it doesn't burn too much. Remove/Extract the pan from the oven and set it aside to cool so the sugar can solidify.
5. Finish with a dollop of vanilla bean cream.

Vanilla bean cream:
1. Mix coconut cream, maple syrup, and vanilla/vanilla bean paste with a hand mixer until well mixed.

Assemble:
1. Drizzle vanilla bean cream over two banana halves on a dish.
2. Serve right away.

Nutrition: Calories: 981 g Carbs: 153.3 g Protein: 9.6 g Fat: 36.6 g

85. Frozen Watermelon Yogurt Pops

Preparation Time: 5 minutes   **Freezing time:** 2 hours   **Servings:** 6 people

INGREDIENTS

- 100 g Greek yogurt
- A drizzle of honey or maple syrup, optional
- 1 round slice of seedless watermelon
- 6 lolly sticks

DIRECTIONS

1. If using, pour honey or maple syrup over the yogurt in a small bowl. To make sure everything is mixed, give it a good stir.
2. Cut the watermelon round into 6 triangles that are about equal in size.
3. Cut a triangle in the center of every piece with a tiny sharp knife and remove it.
4. Cut a slice into each watermelon slice using a sharp knife to create a slice for the pitch stick. Insert a lolly stick into every slice of watermelon.
5. Place the melon slices on a tray or dish that has been lined. Before you start, double-check that the tray will fit in your freezer.
6. Fill the empty triangle within every watermelon piece with a tbsp of yogurt. If necessary, tap the tray on your workbench to ensure that the yogurt fills beneath the lolly stick as well, then top off every slice with a bit extra yogurt.
7. Place the yogurt in the fridge for at least 2 hours or up overnight.
8. When the melon pops are frozen, carefully take them off the tray, set them on a dish at room temperature for a few minutes to soften, and serve immediately.

Nutrition: Calories: 277 g Carbs: 38 g Protein: 8.8 g Fat: 9.9 g

86. Honeydew Melon and Cilantro Ice Pops

Preparation Time: 5 minutes **Cooking Time:** 5 minutes **Servings:** 4 to 6

INGREDIENTS

- cup sugar
- 1 large bunch of cilantro, stems, and leaves roughly chopped (about 1 packed cup)
- 3 cups of 1-inch cubes of honeydew melon
- Zest and juice of one lime (about 1 tsp zest and 2 tbsp juice)
- 1 tbsp kosher salt

DIRECTIONS

1. Specialized gear: 4 or 6 ice-pop sticks, four 4-oz ice-pop molds, or six 3-oz molds.
2. Bring the sugar and ¼ cup water to a simmer in a small frying pan. Over moderate heat, cook, occasionally stirring, until the sugar is completely melted, approximately 5 minutes. Extract the pan from the heat and stir the cilantro, constantly stirring until it has completely wilted. Allow the mixture to, for at least 30 minutes, cool to room temperature.
3. Combine the melon, lime zest, juice, and a pinch of salt in a blender. Pour the cilantro syrup into a blender and, using the back of a spoon, press the cilantro through the strainer to extract as much flavor as possible; discard the cilantro. Halfway through, scrape down the sides of the blender to make the melon mixture completely smooth. Transfer a large liquid measuring cup with the mixture and a pouring spout.
4. Fill the molds halfway with the mixture, leaving ¼ inch of room at the top (the mixture will expand). Place the sticks in place. Freeze for 5 hours overnight until solid. Unmold and eat right away.

Nutrition: Calories: 578 g Carbs: 127.3 g Protein: 7 g Fat: 4.6 g

87. Easy Turkey Meatloaf

Preparation Time: 5 minutes **Cooking Time:** 25 minutes **Servings:** 6

INGREDIENTS

- 18 oz ground turkey breast
- 3 carrots, peeled and grated
- 1 egg beaten
- 1 tbsp soy sauce
- 1 tbsp Dijon mustard
- 1 tsp fish sauce
- 1 tsp dried thyme
- 1 tsp dried rosemary

DIRECTIONS

1. Preheat the oven to 350°F.
2. Mix the turkey, carrots, egg soy sauce, mustard, fish sauce, thyme, and rosemary in a large bowl. Evenly divide the meat-loaf mixture among the cups of a nonstick 6-muffin tin.
3. Bake for about 25 minutes until cooked through.
4. Tip: Spread 1 tsp of tomato sauce over each meatloaf before baking.

Nutrition: Calories: 862 g Carbs: 29.9 g Protein: 98.2 g Fat: 39 g

88. Apple and Spinach Salad

Preparation Time: 5 minutes **Cooking Time:** 25 minutes **Servings:** 6

INGREDIENTS

- ½ tbsp maple syrup
- 1 handful of chopped walnuts
- 1 apple
- 1 tbsp balsamic vinegar
- 1 tbsp sea salt
- 3 handfuls of spinach and salad
- ½ tbsp olive oil
- 1 celery stalk

DIRECTIONS

1. After the apple has been cored, finely slice it.
2. Chop the celery very finely.
3. Combine celery, apples, and cleaned spinach in a large mixing bowl.
4. Combine the vinaigrette and sea salt on a separate plate.
5. Mix the salad ingredients in the bowl after adding the vinaigrette.
6. Serve immediately or store in the fridge for up to a week. Add some chopped walnuts if nuts are okay with your GERD and acid reflux.

Nutrition: Calories: 314 g Carbs: 26.7 g Protein: 3.7 g Fat: 21.2 g

89. Vanilla Frappe

Preparation Time: 5 minutes **Cooking Time:** 0 minutes **Servings:** 6

INGREDIENTS

- 2 ½ cups milk, approximately
- 1 tsp vanilla extract
- 2 tsp sugar
- 2 maraschino cherries or whipped cream, if desired, for garnish

DIRECTIONS

1. Fill an ice cube tray halfway with milk and place it in the freezer for at least 2 hours (overnight works too).
2. Mix the milk cubes, ½ cup milk, vanilla extract, and sugar in a high-powered smoothie blender. Puree before all of the ice cubes are broken down, and the mixture resembles a creamy milkshake.
3. Pour into serving glasses and, if necessary, garnish. Enjoy right now.

Nutrition: Calories: 503 g Carbs: 59.9 g Protein: 18.3 g Fat: 19.8 g

90. Vanilla Ice Cream

Preparation Time: 30 minutes **Cooking Time:** 5 minutes **Servings:** 4

INGREDIENTS

- ¾ cup white sugar
- 1 cup heavy whipping cream
- 2 ¼ cups milk
- 2 tsp vanilla extract

DIRECTIONS

1. Mix the cream, sugar, and milk in a pan and cook over low heat until the sugar has dissolved. Heat until the mixture is steaming hot and a tiny ring of foam forms around the edge.
2. Fill a pourable container with the cream mixture, such as a large measuring cup. Add the vanilla extract and refrigerate the mixture for at least 2 hours. (It's better to leave it overnight.)
3. Pour the chilled ice cream mix into an ice cream maker, set it on, and churn for 20 to 25 minutes, depending on the package recommendations.
4. Serve immediately when the ice cream is lightly frozen, wrap it in plastic wrap, and leave it in the freezer for 2 to 3 hours to ripen.

Nutrition: Calories: 831 g Carbs: 165.5 g Protein: 5 g Fat: 14 g

91. Hamp Seed and Banana Green Smoothie

Preparation Time: 5 minutes **Cooking Time:** 0 minutes **Servings:** 4

INGREDIENTS

- 1 ½ cup fresh spinach leaves, packed
- ¼ cup hulled hemp seeds
- 1 cup chilled coconut water or more to thin
- 1-inch knob of ginger, peeled
- ½ cup frozen banana slices
- 1 cup frozen pineapple chunks

DIRECTIONS

1. In a blender, mix all of the components. Puree until completely smooth.

Nutrition: Calories: 550 g Carbs: 53.5 g Protein: 17 g Fat: 29.9 g

Licorice contains phyto complexes with protective and healing activity of the gastric mucosa.

Tasty Dinner with Friends

92. Frozen Berry and Gingernut Yogurt Pops

Preparation Time: 10 minutes **Cooking Time:** 0 minutes **Servings:** 5

INGREDIENTS

- 100 g ginger nut biscuits
- 405 g can light condensed milk
- 250 g red berries, we used strawberries, raspberries, and redcurrants
- 500 g pot 0% fat natural Greek yogurt
- 250 g purple berries, we used blueberries, blackberries, and blackcurrants
- 8 paper cups
- 8 wooden lolly sticks

DIRECTIONS

1. The biscuits should be ground into crumbs in a mixer. Add 2 tbsp of condensed milk and mix until the crumbs start to clump. With the back of a spoon, spread the crumbs onto each of the eight paper cups. You won't need to make the processor before moving on to the next step if you scrape out every last piece.
2. It is advisable to roughly chop any large berries. Half of the red berries, half of the remaining condensed milk, and half of the yogurt should be blended together until smooth in a mixer. Remove the blade from the processor, then add the remaining chopped red berries. The mixture should be divided among the four paper cups. Repeat with the remaining

ingredients and purple berries.
3. To help each cup stand upright, insert a lollipop stick into the base of the biscuit in each one. Sprinkle at least four hours before serving. To get the lollipops out of the cups, place them upside down on the counter and gently squeeze them until they fall out.

Nutrition: Calories: 2346 g Carbs: 376.3 g Protein: 88.1 g Fat: 54.3 g

93. Chia Seed Pudding

Preparation Time: 40 minutes **Cooking Time:** 0 minutes **Servings:** 6

INGREDIENTS

- 1 cup vanilla-flavored unsweetened almond milk
- 1 cup plain low-fat (2 percent) Greek yogurt
- 2 tbsp pure maple syrup (preferably grade B), + 2 tsp for serving one tsp pure vanilla extract
- 1 tbsp Kosher salt
- ¼ cup chia seeds
- 1 pint strawberries, hulled and chopped
- ¼ cup sliced almonds, toasted
- tofu

DIRECTIONS

1. Lightly whisk the almond milk, tofu, 2 tsp maple syrup, vanilla, and tsp salt together in a medium mixing bowl until only mixed. Mix in the chia seeds and set them aside for 30 minutes. If the roots have settled, stir them to re-distribute them. Refrigerate overnight, covered.
2. Toss the berries with the remaining 4 tsp maple syrup in a medium bowl the next day. Add the almonds and mix well.
3. Serve the pudding in 4 bowls or glasses, topped with a mound of berry mixture.

Nutrition: Calories: 1070 g Carbs: 117.4 g Protein: 50.6 g Fat: 40.4 g

94. Immunity-Boosting Soup

Preparation Time: 10 minutes   **Cooking Time:** 30 minutes   **Servings:** 4

INGREDIENTS

- 1 cup mushrooms
- 1 zucchini
- 1 onion
- 1 tbsp grape seed oil

Recommended herbs:
- 1 tbsp sea salt
- 1 pack of approved spelt flour noodles
- 4 cups water

DIRECTIONS

1. Cook the noodles as directed on the package.
2. The onion is sautéed in a wide skillet of hot grape seed oil until it becomes translucent.
3. Chop the mushroom pieces into small pieces. Cook it in the pan as well. Grated zucchini is added to the pan.
4. Sea salt and water are added. Bring it to a boil over medium heat.
5. Once the boiling point is achieved, reduce the heat. incorporate the cooked noodles.
6. Give it another 15 minutes or so to boil.
7. Serve topped with more herbs and lime juice.

Nutrition: Calories: 1952 g Carbs: 346.8 g Protein: 76.9 g Fat: 28.5 g

95. Low Acid Almond Raspberry Cobbler

Preparation Time: 10 minutes **Cooking Time:** 45 minutes **Servings:** 6

INGREDIENTS

Berries:
- 7 to 8 cups berries (mixed) (strawberries, raspberries, blueberries, and blackberries)
- tsp maple syrup
- 2 tbsp arrowroot starch (or cornstarch or gluten-free flour)

Crisp:
- 1 cup almond flour (or almond meal)
- ⅔ cup of shredded or desiccated coconut (or sub-almond flour or rolled oats if OK with grains)
- 1 cup roughly chopped pecans (or another nut of choice)
- ½ cup coconut sugar
- ½ tsp sea salt
- 4 tbsp coconut oil or vegan butter
- 2 tbsp maple syrup

DIRECTIONS

1. Preheat the oven to 350°F (176°C) and place the fruit in a 9×13 inch or similar-sized cake pan. Toss in the maple syrup and arrowroot until everything is well mixed.
2. Mix the almond flour, coconut, pecans, coconut sugar, and salt in a large bowl.
3. To mix, stir everything together. Then, stir in the coconut oil (or vegan butter) until equally spread using a spoon or your hands. Test a small amount to check whether it's sweet enough.
4. Add additional coconut sugar or a tiny amount of maple syrup (I added 2 tbsp (30 ml) more maple syrup/amount as indicated in the original recipe).
5. Over the fruit, evenly distribute the crisp topping. Cook for 42 to 45 minutes, uncovered, on the middle oven rack, or until the fruit is bubbling and the top is golden brown.
6. Allow 10 minutes for cooling before serving. Serve with coconut whipped cream or coconut vanilla ice cream, if desired. Refrigerate leftovers for up to 4 days if covered.

Nutrition: Calories: 4074 g Carbs: 435.3 g Protein: 60.3 g Fat: 232.5 g

96. Barbecued Rump of Beef in Dijon

Preparation Time: 10 minutes   **Cooking Time:** 2 hours 15 minutes   **Servings:** 4

INGREDIENTS

- 1 kg beef top rump joint
- 2 tbsp fresh tarragon, roughly chopped
- 1 tbsp Dijon mustard
- 1 tbsp olive oil
- 2 tbsp wine vinegar, either red or white

DIRECTIONS

1. Remove the beef joint from its packaging, remove the threads, and discard the extra piece of roasting fat. Make a horizontal incision across the joint's middle without cutting through it, then fold back the 2 sides to form one large, flat piece.
2. In a big, shallow dish, place the meat. Mix the tarragon, mustard, and olive oil in a marinade and massage it all over the meat. Refrigerate for 1 ½ hours, then rub in the vinegar and set aside for 20 minutes.
3. Cook on a medium-hot grill for 15 minutes on every side, then rest for 10 minutes before carving.

Nutrition: Calories: 1181 g Carbs: 1 g Protein: 218.8 g Fat: 33.6 g

97. Pasta With Walnut Pesto

Preparation Time: 15 minutes   **Cooking Time:** 12 minutes   **Servings:** 3

INGREDIENTS

- 400 g pasta (I used orecchiette)
- 175 g walnut halves or pieces
- A handful of fresh basil leaves roughly torn, + extra to serve (optional)
- 100 g parmesan (or vegetarian alternative), freshly grated, + extra to serve (optional)
- 50 g butter
- 4 tbsp extra-virgin olive oil
- 50 ml double cream

DIRECTIONS

1. Bring the spaghetti to a boil. Meanwhile, blitz the walnuts until finely minced in a food processor. Pulse a couple more times with the basil, cheese, butter, and oil. Season.
2. Warm the cream by pouring it into a pan. We should add of the pesto, then gently heated it to release it. Drain the pasta, reserving 2 tbsp of the cooking water, and mix it with the sauce. Serve immediately with more Parmesan and basil. Pesto keeps for a week in the fridge.

Nutrition: Calories: 4083 g Carbs: 345.8 g Protein: 106.8 g Fat: 252.7 g

98. Dill Rye Bread

Preparation Time: 20 minutes
Cooking Time: 40 minutes
Rising time: 1 hour 45 minutes
Servings: 2

INGREDIENTS

- 1 tbsp dry, active yeast
- 2 cups warm water
- 1 tbsp molasses
- 1 tbsp salt
- 1 egg
- 2 tsp caraway seeds
- 2 tsp dill seeds
- 2 cups of dark rye flour
- 3 cups of unbleached all-purpose flour

DIRECTIONS

1. Mix the warm water, molasses, and yeast in a large mixing bowl. Allow 10 minutes for the foam to form.
2. Mix the salt, eggs, seeds, and rye flour in a mixing bowl. Stirring constantly until everything is well mixed.
3. Begin adding the bread flour one cup at a time, mixing well after every addition until a soft dough forms.
4. Knead the dough on a floured surface until it is soft and elastic.
5. Turn the dough in the bowl to coat it in oil. Cover the bowl with a cloth and let rise for approximately an hour or until doubled in size.
6. Grease 2 baking sheets or two bread pans
7. Turn out the dough onto a floured surface after punching it down.
8. Knead the dough lightly and split it in half.
9. Form the dough into two loaves, either in a bread pan or on a baking sheet in rounds/logs.
10. Allow 45 minutes for the dough to rise after being covered with a towel.
11. Preheat the oven to 375°F in the meantime.
12. Bake the bread for 37 to forty minutes in a preheated oven or brown and hollow when tapped with a knuckle.
13. Before slicing, remove the pans from the oven and cool thoroughly on wire racks.

Nutrition: Calories: 2201 g Carbs: 365.2 g Protein: 67.4 g Fat: 52.3 g

99. Ginger Applesauce

Preparation Time: 10 minutes **Cooking Time:** 50 minutes **Servings:** 10

INGREDIENTS

- 4 large Granny Smith apples
- 4 large Red Delicious apples
- 1 cup water
- 1 cup granulated sugar
- 2 tbsp fresh grated ginger pulp

DIRECTIONS

1. 8 apples should be peeled, cored, and cut. Please place them in a container large enough to hold a few inches of apples.
2. Always stir while bringing the apples, water, and sugar to a boil. Set the saucepan's temperature to a low simmer and cover it. For about 10 minutes, cover the pan to steam the apples.
3. With the cover off, start chopping the apples with a wooden fork.
4. Cook the apples for about 40 minutes on low heat or until they are very soft. As the apple chunks cook, keep stirring them and breaking them up into smaller pieces. Don't break down this chunky applesauce too much; simply divide it into small, bite-sized pieces.
5. Add the freshly prepared ginger pulp after the applesauce has finished cooking. Once all of the ginger has been added, thoroughly mix it into the applesauce.
6. Allow the applesauce to cool to room temperature before storing it in the refrigerator.

Nutrition: Calories: 1549 g Carbs: 374 g Protein: 3 g Fat: 4.5 g

100. Maple Pumpkin Custard

Preparation Time: 15 Minutes **Cooking Time:** 25 Minutes **Servings:** 5

INGREDIENTS

- 1 15 oz can puree pumpkin (Make sure that the component is pumpkin alone) or homemade
- ½ cup coconut milk
- ½ cup grade B maple syrup*
- 3 eggs + 1 egg yolk
- 1 tsp vanilla extract
- 1 tsp ground ginger
- 1 tsp ground cinnamon
- ¼ tsp ground clove
- ¼ tsp ground cardamom
- 1 tbsp sea salt

DIRECTIONS

1. Set the oven to 350°F.
2. All the ingredients should be combined in a mixing bowl and whisked until completely smooth and free of lumps.
3. Divide the filling among the individual ramekins about a third of the way full.
4. Place the custards on a rimmed baking sheet and bake for 25 to 30 minutes. They should have a slight wobble in the middle when you remove them.
5. Before freezing, let it reach room temperature for 1 hour.
6. When serving, top with whipped coconut milk cream.

Nutrition: Calories: 895 g Carbs: 90.5 g Protein: 29.8; Fat: 44.6 g

Tasty Dinner with Family

101. Green Pancakes

Preparation Time: 10 minutes   **Cooking Time:** 30 minutes   **Servings:** 4

INGREDIENTS

- ½ cup chickpea flour
- 1 tbsp of your preferred nut butter for additional protein
- ½ tsp sea salt
- 1 tbsp agave syrup
- ½ cup fresh spring water
- 1 burro banana
- ¼ cup blueberries
- 1 handful of amaranth greens

DIRECTIONS

1. All the ingredients should be combined in a mixer until creamy. Avoid using too much water, or they won't cook or get as soft.
2. Allow the batter to rest for around 10 minutes. A non-stick frying pan should be heated over medium-high heat.
3. Scoop the batter into the pan to create six little pancakes. You may change the scale if you'd like. Here, you may make three large pancakes or six little ones.
4. Allow them to cook until the batter begins to bubble and the edges start to appear smooth and cooked. After turning, simmer for a little while longer.
5. Serve with agave syrup, banana burro, and blueberries on top.
6. Enjoy your green pancakes.

Nutrition: Calories: 431 g; Carbs: 61.2 g; Protein: 14.8 g; Fat: 10.8 g.

102. Maple Pancakes

Preparation Time: 5 minutes **Cooking Time:** 10 minutes **Servings:** 6

INGREDIENTS

- 1 cup all-purpose flour
- 1-½ tsp baking powder
- ½ tsp salt
- 1 egg
- 1 cup 2% milk
- 2 tbsp canola oil
- 1 tbsp maple syrup
- Additional maple syrup

DIRECTIONS

1. Whisk the flour and salt in a shallow mixing bowl. Add some baking powder. Mix the egg, milk, oil, and syrup in a separate bowl; whisk into the dry ingredients only until mixed.
2. Pour ¼ cupful of batter onto a hot, lightly greased griddle; transform when bubbles appear on top of pancakes. Cook until golden brown on the second hand (pancakes will be thin). Serve with more syrup on the side.

Nutrition: Calories: 961 g Carbs: 107.6 g Protein: 28.8 g Fat: 46.3 g

103. Mashed Parsnips

Preparation Time: 10 minutes **Cooking Time:** 40 minutes **Servings:** 4

INGREDIENTS

- 5 to 7 fresh sage leaves
- 3 to 4 large parsnips
- 3 to 4 large potatoes (russets are best)
- ½ cup Greek yogurt
- ½ cup butter

DIRECTIONS

1. Peeling parsnips is necessary. If they are quite large, remove the woody core; if they are little, leave them alone.
2. In a dish that can be microwaved, cook for 10 to 12 minutes or until finished.
3. The potatoes should be split in half and boiled for 10 to 15 minutes or until they are tender to the fork.
4. Drain completely.
5. Sauté sage leaves in butter for 1 to 2 minutes.
6. Parsnips and potatoes should be combined in a mixing bowl. Then they should be whipped with an electric mixer or mashed with a potato masher before being combined with sage butter, sour cream, or half-and-half.
7. Blend until the mixture is flawless.

Nutrition: Calories: 2793 g Carbs: 395.3 g Protein: 50.1 g Fat: 112.3 g

104. Blueberry, Chia, Banana and Spinach Smoothie

Preparation Time: 10 minutes **Cooking Time:** 0 minutes **Servings:** 1

INGREDIENTS

- 1 cup orange juice
- 2 generous handfuls of baby spinach
- ¾ cup blueberries frozen
- 1 banana frozen or fresh
- ½ cup ice
- 1 tsp chia seeds

DIRECTIONS

1. In a mixer, combine all ingredients in the order specified, except for chia seeds. Completely smooth to blend. Blend in the chia seeds one more time. Serve right away. (If you let the smoothie rest for too long before drinking it, the chia seeds will thicken it.)
2. This smoothie was rich and delicious, and we all enjoyed it. My sons thoroughly enjoyed eating theirs with spoons.

Nutrition: Calories: 282 g Carbs: 51.4 g Protein: 6.7 g Fat: 5.4 g

105. Easy Homemade Vanilla Pudding

Preparation Time: 25 minutes **Cooking Time:** 10 minutes **Servings:** 4

INGREDIENTS

- ⅓ cup granulated sugar
- 3 tbsp cornstarch
- ⅛ tsp salt
- 2 ¼ cups whole milk
- 2 large egg yolks
- 1 tbsp unsalted butter
- 1-½ tsp pure vanilla extract

DIRECTIONS

1. Mix the milk, egg yolks, maize starch, sugar, and salt in a medium casserole. Cook over medium-low heat, whisking periodically (every minute or two) until the sauce is bubbling all over (this took 7 to 8 minutes for minutes).
2. Once it comes to a boil, cook for an additional one to 2 minutes, stirring occasionally but not vigorously (this can break down the binding properties). The pudding has to be thickened but still soluble at this point; as it cools further, it will get thicker.
3. Remove the butter and vanilla extract from the pan after turning off the heat.
4. These are your options for removing lumps: A fine-mesh strainer should be placed over a large, heatproof basin. Via the sieve, transfer the mixture into the basin. Skip this step if your pudding is lump-free.
5. Put the pudding in either a large mixing bowl or many serving bowls. After cooling to lukewarm, wrap in plastic wrap. Refrigerate for a few hours or until very cold.

Nutrition: Calories: 731 g Carbs: 99 g Protein: 11.7 g Fat: 31.1 g

106. Baked Apples With Tahini Raisin Filling

Preparation Time: 10 minutes   **Cooking Time:** 35 minutes   **Servings:** 4

INGREDIENTS

- 4 ripe apples, cored
- ¾ cup tahini
- 1 cup apple juice
- 3 tbsp raisins
- ⅓ cup chopped pecans
- ¼ tsp cinnamon
- Dash of vanilla
- ¾ cup boiling water

DIRECTIONS

1. Set the oven to 375°F to preheat. Grease a 9x13-inch baking dish with oil.
2. Place the cored apples in the shallow dish.
3. Mix tahini with half a cup of apple juice in a small bowl.
4. Stir in pecans, raisins, vanilla, and cinnamon. Mix well.
5. Stuff this mixture into the core of the apples.
6. Add some boiling water to the baking dish.
7. Pour the remaining apple juice on top.
8. Bake for 35 minutes until tender.
9. Serve the apples with the remaining juices on top.

Nutrition: Calories: 1910 g Carbs: 149 g Protein: 39.7 g Fat: 128.2 g

107. Vanilla Parfait

Preparation Time: 10 minutes   **Cooking Time:** 0 minutes   **Servings:** 2

INGREDIENTS

- 1 cup vanilla milk (unsweetened)
- 1 cup Greek yogurt (plain low-fat)
- 2 tbsp agave
- 1 tsp vanilla
- ⅛ tsp kosher salt
- ¼ cup chia seeds
- 2 cups sliced strawberries
- ¼ cup sliced almonds
- 4 tsp agave for serving

DIRECTIONS

1. Mix milk, yogurt, agave, vanilla, and salt in a medium bowl.
2. Whisk in chia seeds and let them rest for 25 minutes.
3. Cover the bowl and refrigerate it overnight.
4. Mix strawberries with agave and toasted almonds in a bowl.
5. Layer the serving glasses with yogurt pudding and strawberries alternatively.
6. Serve.

Nutrition: Calories: 1240 g; Carbs: 159.1 g; Protein: 48.6 g; Fat: 45.6 g.

108. Pumpkin Pudding Parfaits

Preparation Time: 10 minutes   **Cooking Time:** 22 minutes   **Servings:** 6

INGREDIENTS

- 1 cup pumpkin puree
- ¼ cup packed Splenda
- ½ tsp ground cinnamon
- 3 cups almond milk
- 2 tbsp almond butter
- ½ cup Splenda
- 3 tbsp xanthan gum
- 1 tsp salt
- 4 large egg whites
- 2 tsp vanilla extract

DIRECTIONS

1. Mix pumpkin puree with cinnamon and eggs in a saucepan.
2. Stir and cook the mixture for 10 minutes until smooth.
3. Heat 2 cups of milk with almond butter in a microwave for 2 minutes on high heat.
4. Whisk Splenda with salt and xanthan gum in a large pan.
5. Stir in 1 cup milk and mix well until smooth.
6. Cook until the mixture thickens.
7. Stir in vanilla and strain the mixture.
8. Add half of the vanilla pudding to the pumpkin mixture.
9. Mix well and divide the pumpkin pudding into serving cups.
10. Top the pumpkin pudding with the remaining vanilla pudding.
11. Refrigerate for 4 hours.
12. Garnish as desired and serve.

Nutrition: Calories: 668 g Carbs: 55.3 g Protein: 31.4 g Fat: 27.9 g

Nutritional values given are for the entire recipe, not per individual serving.

Chapter 6
Meal Plan

DAYS	BREAKFAST	LUNCH	DINNER	SNACK	DESSERT
1	Blueberry and spinach superfood green smoothie	Carrot-ginger salad	Steamer clams with bacon and fennel	Almond meringue cookies	Detox berries smoothie
2	Yogurt and fruit parfaits	Squash soup	Miso-glazed scallops	Peanut butter cookies	Cranberry smoothie
3	Pear, ginger, and almond yogurt parfait	Flank steak	Mashed parsnips	Blueberry cherry crisp	Apple ginger smoothie
4	Apple and linseed porridge	Marinated lamb steaks	Mashed cauliflower potatoes	Roasted bananas with brown sugar-walnut glaze	Coconut flour cupcakes
5	Acid reflux smoothie	Mediterranean Pizza	Grilled vegetable pasta salad	Maple syrup and banana sauce	Heart-healthy smoothie
6	Yogurt parfait with pear and ginger	Oven blasted vegetables	Baked potato soup	Baked Indian pudding with maple syrup	Magnesium-boosting smoothie
7	Banana almond flax smoothie	Irish baked potato soup	Summer vegetable kebabs	Cool cucumber soup	Detox berries smoothie
8	Omega overnight oats	Barbecued rump of beef in dijon	Mediterranean green beans	High protein kidney bean salad	Cinnamon berry smoothie
9	Baked apples with cinnamon and ginger	Pasta with walnut pesto	Sweet and crunchy coleslaw	Lighter apple and pear pie	Cranberry smoothie
10	Mexican breakfast toast	Vegan Mexican cheese pourable	Lamb stew with olives	Peach and blueberry yogurt cake	Apple almond smoothie

11	Banana breakfast pudding	Crispy oven-baked chicken tenders	Steak with onion	Green yogurt kick	Apple ginger smoothie
12	Papaya breakfast boat	Roast rib of beef	Creamy herb mushroom chicken	Whole wheat donuts	Coconut flour cupcakes
13	Corn porridge with maple and raisins	Rosemary broiled shrimp	Ginger honeydew soup	Zucchini hummus	Magnesium-boosting smoothie
14	Broccoli omelet	Turkey stew	Immunity-boosting soup	No-bake energy balls	Heart-healthy smoothie

Conclusion

Thank you for reading this acid reflux cookbook. There are a lot of people who suffer in silence or ignore the symptoms of acid reflux. Ignoring it is the worst thing you could do. It could lead to more serious issues in the future. This is nothing to be ashamed of. This book contains not only information about acid reflux but also recipes and a meal plan. The most difficult aspect of making a lifestyle change is getting started. I wanted to make the process a little easier by providing you with the information you need to get started. You can get started right away without having to do a lot of planning.

Acid reflux is a stomach or digestive disorder that causes irritation and agitation in a person. Poor digestion, improper food intake, lack of sleep, and inactivity are the primary causes of this problem. Acid reflux can be caused by an increase in obesity and other health complications. A person suffering from this chronic disorder experiences heartburn and the sensation that their food is not being properly digested. If not treated properly, it can lead to further health complications such as cancer or ulcers. To get immediate relief from acid reflux, make dietary changes such as eating small meals instead of large ones, starting an exercise routine, avoiding citrus, limiting spicy and fried foods, and losing weight. Acid reflux can be treated and prevented in its early stages by eating healthy and organic foods. A proper medical examination is also required to determine the severity of the problem. Consulting doctors and following their advice on treatment and precautions is a necessary step in avoiding gastric acid reflux.

We all want to be able to live our lives free of the pain caused by acid reflux. It's not only painful, but it's also inconvenient. You should leave fully equipped with the knowledge you need to start living a healthier lifestyle.

Good luck

Jude Arson

Conversion Table

VOLUME EQUIVALENTS (LIQUID)

US STANDARD	US STANDARD (OUNCES)	METRIC (APPROXIMATE)
2 tablespoons	1 fl. oz.	30 mL
1/4 cup	2 fl. oz.	60 mL
1/2 cup	4 fl. oz.	120 mL
1 cup	8 fl. oz.	240 mL
1-1/2 cup	12 fl. oz.	355 mL
2 cups or 1 pint	16 fl. oz.	475 mL
4 cups or 1 quart	32 fl. oz.	1 L
1 gallon	128 fl. oz.	4 L

VOLUME EQUIVALENTS (DRY)

US STANDARD	METRIC (APPROXIMATE)
1/8 teaspoon	0.5 mL
1/4 teaspoon	1 mL

1/2 teaspoon	2 mL
3/4 teaspoon	4 mL
1 teaspoon	5 mL
1 tablespoon	15 mL
1/4 cup	59 mL
1/3 cup	79 mL
1/2 cup	118 mL
2/3 cup	156 mL
3/4 cup	177 mL
1 cup	235 mL
2 cups or 1 pint	475 mL
3 cups	700 mL
4 cups or 1 quart	1 L

OVEN TEMPERATURES

FAHRENHEIT (F)	CELSIUS (C) (APPROXIMATE)
250°	120°
300°	150°
325°	165°
350°	180°
375°	190°
400°	200°
425°	220°
450°	230°

WEIGHT EQUIVALENTS

US STANDARD	METRIC (APPROXIMATE)
1/2 ounce	15 g
1 ounce	30 g
2 ounces	60 g
4 ounces	115 g
8 ounces	225 g
12 ounces	340 g
16 ounces or 1 pound	455 g

Printed in Great Britain
by Amazon